JONNI McCOY

Healthy MEALS

FOR LESS

Great-Tasting Simple Recipes
Under $1 a Serving

BETHANYHOUSE
MINNEAPOLIS, MINNESOTA

Published by Bethany House Publishers
11400 Hampshire Avenue South
Bloomington, Minnesota 55438

Bethany House Publishers is a division of
Baker Publishing Group, Grand Rapids, Michigan

Library of Congress Cataloging-in-Publication Data

McCoy, Jonni
    Healthy meals for less : great-tasting simple recipes under $1 a serving / Jonni McCoy.
      p. cm.
    Rev. ed. of: Miserly meals, c2002.
    Includes index.
    Sumary: "Over 200 easy-to-prepare delicious and nutritious recipes, from main dishes to desserts, can be made for less than one dollar per serving"—Provided by publisher.
    ISBN 978-0-7642-0710-5 (pbk. : alk. paper) 1. Low budget cookery. I. McCoy, Jonni. Miserly meals. II. Title.
    TX652.M194   2009
    641.5'52—dc22

                                                    2009025130

ACKNOWLEDGMENTS

Special thanks are due to my husband, Beau,
for his unwavering faith in my ability to
help others through my writing.
A special hug goes to my children, Jeremy and Jessica,
for their patience, support, and willingness to try new recipes.
I owe my mom, Joan Stivers, particular thanks
for instilling in me at an early age the delight in cooking.

I want to give a special thanks to my test chefs,
who spent numerous hours testing these recipes.
Your help made them even better!

Cheryl Coffin, esq.
Melissa Filkins
Mindy Harrington
Vickilynn Haycraft
Maria Irizarry
Kathy Merrill
Kat Osten
Kristen Paris
Donna Salinas
Lori Scott
Julie Shirin
Debbie Steele
Joan Stivers
Michele Woodland

JONNI MCCOY holds a Bachelor of Arts degree in Speech Communication from the University of California at Santa Barbara. Prior to motherhood, she spent ten years as a senior buyer and supervisor for electronics firms such as Apple Computer and National Semiconductor. She presents seminars on living for less to women's groups and other conferences. She has been practicing her frugal ways since 1991. Jonni has appeared on the *Gayle King Show* and *The 700 Club* and radio programs such as *Focus on the Family, FamilyLife Today,* and the *Dick Staub Show.* She has also been featured in *The Wall Street Journal, Good Housekeeping, Woman's World, Family Circle, Family Fun, Working Mother,* and *Woman's Day* magazines, and online at *Oprah.com, Dr. Laura .com, CBS.Marketwatch.com,* and *SmartMoney.com.* Jonni and her family make their home in Colorado Springs, Colorado.

FOR MORE HELP with recipes and money-saving tips, visit *www.miserlymoms .com.* We offer numerous resources for the frugal person (or frugal wannabe). There are articles, links to other money-saving sites, discussion groups, and much more. Drop by soon!

www.miserlymoms.com

CONTENTS

Why This Cookbook Is Different

"YOUR IDEALS ARE WELL WITHIN YOUR REACH."
—ANCIENT CHINESE PROVERB

When I first embarked on my frugal lifestyle, we found most of the extra savings we needed to pay other bills within the grocery budget. We were able to reduce our food bill by more than half! Part of that reduction was through smarter shopping techniques. In my book *Miserly Moms*, I explain in great detail how to shop differently in order to reduce your grocery spending. I don't want to repeat those tips here, but rather encourage you to read *Miserly Moms* to learn to stretch your dollar.

Nevertheless, shopping is only part of the way to save grocery money. The other part is to modify the menu. Both things need to be done in order to accomplish a maximum reduction in grocery spending. After all, how can we save money if we have steak several times per week? We need new recipes that call for simple ingredients but still provide an appealing and healthy meal to the family.

That last part of my goal is what this book is really all about. When people hear that I shop and cook frugally, they often assume that our meals are high in carbohydrates, low in protein, and high in fat. It saddens me that there are such misconceptions out there about inexpensive meals.

I want to report that these assumptions don't have to be true, and I will provide numerous examples and options to support my position. This book includes over two hundred recipes that offer several features that no other cookbook offers:

- *Each recipe costs $1 or less per serving.* The cost per serving is indicated on each recipe page.
- *Each recipe has been tested by a chef* to make sure the recipe is written correctly, the servings are accurate, and the flavor is tasty.

- *Each recipe is nutritious* (according to RDA standards) and is backed up by a detailed nutritional analysis.
- *Each recipe offers a preparation time estimate as well as a cook time estimate.*
- *Each recipe is easy to make.* No tricky maneuvers or tools are needed.
- *Each recipe page offers a kitchen tip on varying subjects of interest to a chef.*

Chapter 1, "The Miserly Kitchen," explains these features in greater detail. I have also included some nutritional information that I felt was important to keep your family healthy. Page through the information in "The Miserly Kitchen," read some of the Kitchen Tips, and take a look at the charts at the end of the book to see how you can make your kitchen a more effective place.

Use these recipes as a springboard for your own creative ideas. Perhaps you can change a few of your family's favorite meals to make them healthier and cost less. Perhaps you can branch out and add a few vegetarian meals that everyone will love and benefit from, health wise as well as financially. These recipes are our family's favorites. You may notice the lack of pork recipes. That is because my family doesn't like the taste of pork, and no other reason. You can substitute pork for the beef or chicken called for in many of the recipes.

Many of us are frugal in our cooking because we need that extra grocery money somewhere else; others have a financial goal they are trying to meet and need every extra dime. Regardless of your reasons for reducing your grocery budget, let my recipes be a tool to saving you money for some other goal. Let your frugal cooking be an enhancement to your family's budget, not a frustration.

Bon appetit!

The Miserly Kitchen

HOW TO USE THIS BOOK

Cost Per Serving

Each recipe in this book provides a cost per serving; all are $1 or less. I calculated the cost using good sale prices. I did not include any "once in a blue moon" prices, but just average sale prices obtainable at most supermarkets. Of course, if you do not purchase items on sale or if you avoid generic products, your cost per serving will be higher than mine. For example, if you make the spanish rice (see page 70) and purchase store-brand tomatoes on sale for 69¢ per can and use generic regular rice (not instant rice), you will be able to achieve the suggested cost per serving. If, however, you purchase name-brand tomatoes at the regular retail price and if you use name-brand rice and/or instant rice, your cost per serving could be double or triple what I suggest. Name brands cost more than off brands, and instant rice costs a great deal more than non-instant rice. So how you shop directly affects the cost per serving of these recipes. Prices also vary in different parts of the country.

In my book *Miserly Moms,* I explain how to change the way you shop in order to maximize your grocery dollar. Those shopping tips need to be employed in order to achieve the goal of $1 or less per serving. Buying ingredients when they are on sale, buying off brands, buying in bulk, and cooking from scratch are a few of the key principles I recommend in order to reduce grocery spending. For more help on achieving these suggested costs per serving, please consult that book.

Serving Sizes

The serving size suggested in each recipe is more than sufficient for a nutritionally balanced meal. The sizes meet or exceed the RDA (Recommended Dietary Allowances) guidelines provided by the Food and Nutrition Board.

Many people complain that they need more protein than is recommended. The extra protein may be costing us unnecessarily and may actually be harmful. The American diet has always been heavy on the meat and light on the vegetables and grains. We tend to have a lopsided plate. We are one of the few countries in the world that features the main dish and understates the side dishes. Most countries have what we consider the main dish as the side dish, and the produce and grains are the main attraction. To be more in line with the RDAs for protein, we need to reduce the amount of the main dish on the plate and increase the amount of the vegetables, fruit, and grains. This switch will also help us eat our five servings per day of produce that our bodies need.

Since we add side dishes to main dishes, snack during the day, and add protein-filled drinks to some meals (such as a glass of milk or milk in cereal), we are eating more protein than we may be aware of. Most of us don't realize how much extra protein we add throughout the day with side dishes. For example, the zesty low-fat fries (see page 65) have 4 grams of protein per serving, the corn soufflé (see page 73) has 8 grams of protein per serving, and 1 cup of steamed broccoli has 5 grams of protein. These three side dishes provide 17 of the 50 grams of protein the average adult needs per day.

Nutritional Analysis

A nutritional analysis is provided for each recipe in order for you to evaluate whether the recipe fits within your dietary boundaries. The nutritional values for calories, fat, cholesterol, carbohydrates, fiber, protein, and sodium are included.

Recommended Dietary Allowances (RDA) have been established for each of those categories. Remember that these guidelines are designed for the average healthy adult and vary based on height, weight, and special health needs:

Calories—2000
Fat—65 grams
Cholesterol—300 mg
Carbohydrates—300 grams
Fiber—25 grams
Protein—50 grams
Sodium—2400 mg (1 teaspoon of salt has 2100 mg)

Kitchen Tip

I have included some helpful information following each recipe. Most of the tips pertain to the recipe they are with. To find a tip quickly, there is an index for tips along with the recipes at the end of this book.

Blue Ribbon

The Blue Ribbon award is given to the one recipe in each chapter that is the most nutritionally sound as well as the cheapest per serving. Since the focus of this book is to offer cheap but healthy meals, I wanted to point out the best of the best to you.

Abbreviations

The following abbreviations are used in this book:

lb. = pound   mg = milligram
oz. = ounce   qt. = quart
T. = tablespoon   tsp. = teaspoon

High-Altitude Adjustments

These recipes do not include high-altitude adjustments. If you live at high altitude (3,000 feet or above), you will need to make the following adjustments.

For Baking:

- Raise the temperature about 25 degrees.
- Reduce the baking powder by ¼ teaspoon for each teaspoon called for.
- Reduce the sugar by 1 tablespoon for each cup called for.
- Add 1 tablespoon of flour for each cup called for.
- Grease and flour pans well since cakes and breads tend to stick more to pans at high altitudes.

For Candy Making:

Boiling temperatures are lower at higher altitudes. Water boils at 212 degrees at sea level but at 203 degrees at 5,000 feet, and at still lower temperatures as the altitude gets higher.

Since the temperature varies with the altitude, it is best to check the syrup with the "water test" instead of relying on a thermometer. The water test consists of dropping ½ teaspoon of hot syrup into a glass of cool tap water.

- The soft-ball stage has been reached if the syrup drops into a ball that you can pick up but it flattens right away.
- The hard-ball stage has been reached when you can pick up the ball and it stays a ball in your fingers.
- The hard-crack stage has been reached when streaks of syrup form as the syrup drops and they are brittle, breaking when they hit the bottom of the glass.

For further help with high-altitude cooking, consult your favorite cooking reference book or do a search on the Web for "high-altitude cooking" or "high-altitude baking."

PANTRY BASICS

Every pantry needs a few staple items. Even if you don't have the much-coveted walk-in pantry, having these items in a cupboard will make your cooking much easier. And it will save you money as well: cooking a meal costs significantly less than ordering take-out or buying a frozen meal. Add to that the savings you will get by having staples on hand that were bought on sale, and you'll be even further ahead. If you need more space than is available in your cupboard, consider converting a small closet into a pantry. Some homes have a broom closet that can be converted by adding some shelves.

I have tried to include the items I have in my kitchen. Of course, your family may prefer different or additional items, so use this as a framework to build around. The items I have listed are items that are used often in the recipes in this book. I have not included items that are used only occasionally.

Equipment

- Good sharp knives are a must.
- Good cutting board to preserve the integrity of your knives. I prefer wood, and recent studies show that wood cutting boards harbor fewer bacteria than plastic boards. With hot water, antibacterial soap, and a good scrubber, wood cutting boards clean up well.
- Powerful blender. If you have a space problem and have to choose between appliances, a food processor can be used in its place in most cases.
- Mixer for preparing batters and other mixes.
- Heavy non-aluminum skillet. A heavier pan distributes the heat better, making burnt food less likely.
- Cheese grater.
- Several pots of varying sizes: 2 quart, 4 quart, and 6 quart are often used.
- Plastic storage containers. I prefer thick zippered plastic bags for freezing leftovers. They are less expensive than plastic boxes and allow more food to be stored in a limited space.
- Garlic press for crushing fresh garlic.
- Measuring cups and spoons. Don't use regular teaspoons, tablespoons, or cups for measuring, as the sizes vary greatly.
- Meat thermometer.
- Small-screen strainer for straining pulp from juices.
- Large strainer for rinsing and draining pasta and vegetables.

Spices and Seasonings

- Garlic powder
- Powdered ginger
- Cayenne pepper
- Oregano
- Rosemary
- Chili powder
- Ground nutmeg
- Sage
- Onion powder
- Curry powder
- Basil
- Thyme
- Red pepper flakes
- Ground cinnamon
- Paprika
- Parsley

Note: I often call for a spice called *Italian seasoning*. You will find the recipe for this combination of herbs in the "Mixes" chapter. I recommend that you make it and keep it on hand for easy use. If you prefer to buy an Italian seasoning mixture, check the label to make sure it's not loaded with salt: it could spoil the recipe.

Pasta and Grains

- Spaghetti and fettuccine noodles
- Oatmeal
- Long grain rice

Baking Ingredients

- Baking powder
- Cornstarch
- Whole wheat flour
- White sugar

- Baking soda
- White flour
- Unsweetened cocoa
- Brown sugar

Condiments

- Honey
- Soy sauce
- Worcestershire sauce
- Vegetable oil
- Cooking oil spray
- Red wine vinegar

- Tabasco sauce
- Ketchup
- Mayonnaise
- Olive oil
- Cider vinegar
- Dijon mustard

Fresh Produce

- Onions
- Potatoes

- Garlic

In the Refrigerator

- Cheddar cheese
- Milk or soymilk

- Eggs

In the Freezer

- Cooked beans (they freeze great!)
- Cooked rice (also freezes great!)
- Chicken breasts (boneless and skinless are recommended for ease of use and lower fat content)

On the Shelf

- Tuna
- Tomato sauce
- Raisins
- Chicken broth powder (see below)

- Canned diced tomatoes
- Tomato paste
- Lemon juice
- Beef broth powder (see below)

Broth powders

Chicken and beef broth powders are not the same thing as bouillon cubes. Broth powders are made from herbs, spices, and yeast and have little or no salt added. Bouillon tends to be very salty. If bouillon were used where broth powder was called for, the recipe would be too salty. Broth powders can be purchased from health food stores in bulk, and some regular supermarkets also carry it. I prefer to buy it at a health food store because I know those brands have little or no salt added. If you purchase broth powder in a supermarket and it comes in a prepackaged container (not in bulk), read the nutrition label to make sure the sodium content is low. To avoid getting the wrong item and ruining a recipe, I strongly recommend making broth powder yourself; it is very easy and inexpensive (see the recipe for broth powder on page 226). Follow these guidelines when substituting for bouillon, broth powder, or stock:

- If you have only bouillon cubes, and the recipe calls for broth powder, this conversion chart may help:

- *1 cup water + 1 T. broth powder = 1 cup stock*

- *1 T. broth powder + 1 tsp. salt = 2 bouillon cubes*

- If a recipe calls for broth powder and you have only bouillon cubes, you will need to reduce the salt in your recipes. Here is a conversion chart that may help:

- *4 bouillon cubes - 2 tsp. salt (called for in recipe) = 2 T. broth power*

- However, sometimes there is not enough salt called for in the recipe to remove, and the meal will taste salty if a bouillon cube is used in place of broth powder. For example, the meatless meatloaf (page 117) calls for 2 T. broth powder and 1 tsp. of salt. You could use 4 bouillon cubes in place of the broth powder, but only 1 teaspoon of salt is called for in the recipe, when you should remove 2 teaspoons. In this case, you could use only 2 bouillon cubes and omit all salt called for, but the meal will be a bit less flavorful.

- If the recipe calls for liquid broth or stock and all you have is bouillon cubes, omit 1 teaspoon of salt from the recipe (if salt is called for) for every 2 bouillon cubes you use. If the recipe has no salt that you can omit, use less of the bouillon and taste before you add any more so as not to ruin the recipe with too much salt. For example, in hearty minestrone soup (page 50): omit the 15 ounces of broth, omit the ½ tsp. salt, and add to the recipe 2 cups of water and 2 bouillon cubes to start with, tasting before adding the other 2 cubes.

- If all you have is canned broth or stock, and the recipe calls for broth powder or bouillon cubes, replace the water that is called for in the recipe with an equal amount of liquid broth. For example, Jessica's stone soup (page 52) calls for ⅓ cup broth powder and 10 cups water. The broth powder and the water could be omitted and 10 cups of liquid broth could be used instead.

OIL NUTRITION TIPS

If you are anything like me when I go shopping for cooking oil, you get a bit confused at the choices. There are all sorts of nut- and seed-based oils: walnut, peanut, grape seed, sesame, sunflower seed, safflower, flaxseed, cottonseed, canola, corn, and olive to name just a few. All cooking oils come from some seed or nut. Some of the methods used for extraction affect the oil's quality, nutritional value, and taste, and some seeds produce oil that is better at meeting our dietary needs than others.

How do you know which to buy? The following information should help you buy the best for both your recipes and for your health. The recipes in this book rarely call for a specific type of oil, leaving it to the preference of the chef. But I try to use olive oil as often as possible—even in my baking. Breads and muffins do well with oil and do not have to have shortening or butter. However, some recipes will not do as well with oil, such as sugar cookies. To substitute oil for the shortening or butter called for in a recipe, multiply the amount of the solid fat by .75 (that is, use 25% less). For example, if a recipe calls for ¼ cup (4 tablespoons) of shortening or butter, use 3 tablespoons of oil instead.

Extraction

Most oil sold in supermarkets is extracted from the seed or nut in one of two ways: pressing or chemical solvents. Chemical solvent extraction is less desirable. In this process, the seeds or nuts are ground into a pulp, and then soaked in a solvent. Most of the solvent is removed when the oil is boiled. Little is left of the oil's original nutritional value. Pressed oil is a better option, with cold pressed being preferable. The heat in hot pressing can affect the oil's nutritional value, but it is less harmful than the solvents.

The only way to verify if your oil has been mechanically pressed to extract the oil and not chemically treated is to make sure the label says "cold pressed" or "expeller pressed" oil. Extra-virgin olive oil is the oil most likely to be cold pressed and not extracted with solvents (see the following paragraph on olive oil).

Here is a quick overview of the types of oils:

Olive Oil

Olive oil is very easy to digest and is a great addition to the diet. There are two main types: virgin and extra virgin. The differences are noteworthy in both nutrition and health. *Extra virgin* oil is the first oil off of the first pressing of the olives. It is the purest of the olive oils and the lightest tasting. It almost never has the oil extracted by solvents. *Virgin* oil comes from the last pressing of the olive pulp. The pulp may be pressed or, more likely, soaked in solvents to extract the remaining oil. This last pressing tastes the most bitter and has the most impurities. *Light* olive oil is extra virgin olive oil that has been filtered to remove what few impurities it has that give a bitter taste. It is very mild and can be used in baking. *Fino* (fine) olive oil is a blend of extra virgin and virgin olive oil. It has a longer shelf life than regular oils and can be stored for up to six months at room temperature or up to a year in the refrigerator.

Canola Oil

This comes from the little-known rape seed and is the most widely used oil. Its taste is mild and it makes a good cooking or salad oil.

Peanut Oil

Peanut oil is prized by chefs for its high heat tolerance; it is commonly used in restaurants for deep-frying. Its nutty flavor is not overpowering, and it can be used in salads.

Safflower Oil

This oil is less nutritious than many oils since it lacks vitamin E, but it is favored by some chefs because it can tolerate high heat before burning.

Sunflower Oil

This oil burns more easily than safflower oil, but it can still be used for cooking. Its light flavor also makes it a good choice for salads.

Corn Oil

Corn oil is the most versatile and cheapest of the vegetable oils, so it is often used in margarines and salad dressings.

Flaxseed Oil

Flaxseed oil is high in omega-3 fatty acids and vitamin E. It cannot be used for cooking since it cannot tolerate any heat and burns easily. It is used for its nutritional value and can be added to salads, spreads, casseroles, etc.

Storage

All oils can go rancid if exposed to heat or light for prolonged periods. Rancidity changes the nutritional value of the oil as well as the taste. If oil is stored in a closed container in a room kept at 65 degrees or below, it will last for two to three months, with olive oil lasting longer—for up to a year. Since light can affect the nutritional value, it is best to keep oil in a tinted or dark container.

Essential Fatty Acids

Some fats have nutrients called *essential fatty acids* (*EFAs*), which our bodies need for proper functioning. They are often referred to as omega-3 (linolenic) and omega-6 (linoleic) fatty acids. These elements are particularly essential to proper brain function, lowering bad (LDL) cholesterol levels, elevating good (HDL) cholesterol levels, regulating hormones, and converting foods into energy. Our body cannot manufacture EFAs, so they must be obtained from foods regularly. An RDA has not been established for EFAs, but many nutritionists recommend 6,500 milligrams per day. Good sources of EFAs are flaxseed oil, grape seed oil, walnuts, soy, mackerel, sardines, salmon, and tuna. A lack of EFAs can produce varying symptoms, the most frequent being skin problems (on the face in particular) and headaches. If these high-EFA foods aren't your favorites, you can add flaxseed oil to salad dressings or casseroles, mix it with butter as a spread, or take oil supplements. Here is a brief overview of sources of omega-3 fatty acids:

Food Source	Milligrams of Omega-3 Fatty Acids
1 T. flaxseed oil	7,526 mg
¼ cup walnuts	1,034
1 T. wheat germ oil	938
1 T. soybean oil	927
1 T. safflower oil	55

Unsaturated Fats

These are the fats that have a plant source and are liquid when at room temperature. This classification can be broken into two groups: monounsaturated fats and polyunsaturated fats. *Monounsaturated fats* help reduce the bad cholesterol levels (LDLs). The most commonly used monounsaturated fats are canola oil, peanut oil, and olive oil. The *polyunsaturated fats* are considered acceptable fats because they neither add saturated cholesterol-laden fat to the diet, nor do they interfere with good health. These oils include corn oil, safflower oil, soybean oil, and sunflower oil.

Saturated Fats

Most saturated fats come from animal sources and stay solid at room temperature. The exceptions to the animal source are coconut oil and palm oil, which are commonly used in commercial food preparation. Common examples of saturated fat are butter, lard, margarine, and vegetable shortening. They are not recommended in our diet due to their high cholesterol levels and possible cancer-causing effects. The vegetable oil that margarine and shortening are made of is converted into a saturated fat once it is hydrogenated (the transformation of a liquid to a solid by injecting hydrogen atoms into the unsaturated oil, making trans fatty acids).

CHAPTER 2

Appetizers

Seafood Spread

Serves 4
Preparation Time: 15 minutes

- 6-oz. can tuna (or salmon)
- ⅓ cup grated Parmesan cheese
- 1 T. mayonnaise
- ⅛ tsp. curry powder
- 1 tsp. finely chopped onion
- 1 T. finely chopped celery

Combine all of the ingredients until very smooth. Spread on crackers.

For added flavor or texture, add other finely diced vegetables (garlic, bell peppers, etc.), or other spices such as cumin or Tabasco sauce.

Cost per serving (4 tsp.): 42¢

NUTRITIONAL ANALYSIS PER SERVING
Calories: 105
Fat: 5 grams
Cholesterol: 20 mg
Carbohydrates: 1 gram
Fiber: 0 grams
Protein: 14 grams
Sodium: 291 mg

Kitchen Tip

To REDUCE THE FAT in a recipe, substitute a low-fat version of the ingredient. For example, use a low-fat cheese or mayonnaise instead of regular.

Hummus

Serves 12
Preparation Time: 15 minutes

- 2 15-oz. cans garbanzo beans
- 3 cloves garlic, pressed
- 2 T. lemon juice
- ¼ tsp. ground cumin
- ⅛ tsp. salt

After draining the liquid from the garbanzo beans, pour the beans into a blender. Cover and blend for 1 minute. Add remaining ingredients and process until smooth.

Serve this Middle Eastern dish as a dip or spread with raw vegetable slices, crackers, or pita bread.

Options: add ¼ cup tahini (sesame seed paste) and/or 1 cup cooked carrots. Blend these with the beans.

Cost per serving (¼ cup): 13¢

NUTRITIONAL ANALYSIS PER SERVING
Calories: 86
Fat: 1 gram
Cholesterol: 0 mg
Carbohydrates: 16 grams
Fiber: 3 grams
Protein: 3 grams
Sodium: 234 mg

Kitchen Tip

Use a pepper mill to GRIND SPICES such as cloves, celery seeds, coriander, or caraway, or any hard and dry spice. Freshly ground spices will add more flavor than the pre-ground version.

Quesadilla

Serves 12
Preparation Time: 15 minutes
Cooking Time: 1 to 2 minutes

- 12 fat-free flour tortillas (7-inch)
- 2 cups grated cheddar cheese

Place the tortillas on a cookie sheet (do this in batches since they won't all fit on one sheet). Sprinkle cheese over them evenly. Place in the oven under the broiler for 1 to 2 minutes. Or heat over medium heat on an ungreased cast iron skillet. Watch them closely, as they burn quickly. Remove from oven and immediately fold the tortillas in half. Cut each into 3 triangles.

Variation: For added flavor, combine a few teaspoons mayonnaise with diced green chilies and Tabasco sauce to taste, and then spread a little on each tortilla before adding cheese. For a low-fat variation, just add salsa (see page 34).

For a main dish, add diced meat to the cheese before baking. For a breakfast dish, add diced sausage or scrambled eggs.

Cost per serving (3 wedges): 24¢

NUTRITIONAL ANALYSIS PER SERVING
Calories: 186
Fat: 1 gram
Cholesterol: 18 mg
Carbohydrates: 20 grams
Fiber: 1 gram
Protein: 8 grams
Sodium: 275 mg

Kitchen Tip

Cooking with CAST IRON will increase your intake of iron, which is beneficial for most of us. To care for your cast iron pans, be sure to coat with vegetable oil after each washing, wiping off any excess before storing. If rust appears on the pan, soak the pan for 5 to 10 minutes in a solution of 2 cups water and 1 tablespoon citric acid (also called vitamin C powder—found at health food stores). After soaking, wash, dry, oil, and store as usual.

Baked Buffalo Wings

Serves 12
Preparation Time: 10 minutes
Cooking Time: 30 minutes

- 2 T. butter, melted
- ¼ cup hot sauce (see page 204)
- 2 T. vinegar, any type
- 5 lbs. chicken wings

In a bowl, mix together melted butter, hot sauce, and vinegar. Dip chicken into mixture. Place on a lightly oiled baking sheet.

Bake 30 minutes at 350°.

Serve with a bowl of buttermilk or bleu cheese dressing for dipping.

Cost per serving (3 wings): 56¢

NUTRITIONAL ANALYSIS PER SERVING

Calories: 244

Fat: 18 grams

Cholesterol: 83 mg

Carbohydrates: 0 grams

Fiber: 0 grams

Protein: 18 grams

Sodium: 93 mg

Kitchen Tip

To easily REMOVE BURNT FOOD from a pan, skillet, or cooking sheet, cover the burnt food with water, add 2 to 3 tablespoons of baking soda, and let it sit overnight. Most food will loosen. In a hurry? Heat the pan to boiling, adding water if it begins to boil dry. Continue until the food is loosened. To avoid burnt-on food, before cooking, line the pan with aluminum foil that can be peeled off and thrown away.

Olive Oil and Herb Dip

Serves 6
Preparation Time: 10 minutes

- 1 tsp. dried rosemary
- 1 tsp. dried basil
- 1 tsp. dried parsley
- 1 tsp. dried oregano
- 1 tsp. dehydrated minced garlic
- ½ tsp. salt
- 1 tsp. black pepper
- ¾ cup olive oil

Combine all of the dry ingredients in a mortar or bowl. Using a pestle (or large wooden spoon), crush the herbs into smaller pieces. Do not put these in a blender. You don't want them too fine.

Place 1 teaspoon of the herb mixture in the center of 6 small plates. Pour 2 tablespoons (more or less to taste) of olive oil over the herbs.

Serve with French bread. Dip the bread into the oil and herbs and enjoy!

Cost per serving (1 tsp. herbs + 2 T. oil): 38¢

NUTRITIONAL ANALYSIS PER SERVING	
Calories: 243	
Fat: 27 grams	
Cholesterol: 0 mg	
Carbohydrates: 1 gram	
Fiber: 0 grams	
Protein: 0 grams	
Sodium: 179 mg	

 Kitchen Tip

DRIED GARLIC can be used in place of fresh garlic in most recipes. It has less flavor but is a good substitute in a pinch. To convert your recipe, use the following guide: 1 clove=1 tsp. fresh chopped=¼ tsp. dried minced= ⅛ tsp. powdered.

Hot Artichoke Dip

Serves 6
Preparation Time: 5 minutes
Cooking Time: 1 hour

- 6-oz. jar marinated artichoke hearts
- 2 T. canned diced green chilies
- ¼ cup mayonnaise
- 1 cup grated cheddar cheese
- 2 cloves garlic, pressed
- ½ tsp. salt

Remove the artichokes from the jar, reserving the liquid for later. Chop the artichoke hearts. In a small slow cooker (don't use a large one) or heavy saucepan, combine everything except the reserved liquid. Cover and cook for 1 hour on low heat (small slow cookers only cook at one temperature). Occasionally stir the ingredients to blend.

After one hour, add 2 tablespoons of the reserved liquid, and stir to mix well.

Serve immediately. Keep the dip on a warming plate or in the small slow cooker.

Serve with tortilla chips or crackers.

Cost per serving (¼ cup): 82¢

NUTRITIONAL ANALYSIS PER SERVING	
Calories:	158
Fat:	14 grams
Cholesterol:	25 mg
Carbohydrates:	4 grams
Fiber:	2 grams
Protein:	6 grams
Sodium:	374 mg

Kitchen Tip

Recipes use different terms for PREPARING GARLIC, but they all mean pretty much the same thing. Whether it's pressed (through a garlic press), crushed (with the flat side of a chef's knife), minced, or finely chopped (with a knife), the result is small bits of fresh garlic. The more cells that are opened in the garlic, the more flavor that is released into the food.

Herbed Cheese Spread

Serves 8
Preparation Time: 10 minutes

- ½ cup chopped fresh parsley
- 1 T. Italian seasoning (see page 209)
- 1 T. ground basil
- 2 cloves garlic, pressed
- 16 oz. low-fat cream cheese, softened
- ¼ cup butter, softened
- 1 tsp. Worcestershire sauce
- ½ tsp. red wine vinegar

Place all of the ingredients in a mixing bowl. Blend with a mixer until smooth and the herbs are evenly distributed.

Serve with crackers and vegetable sticks. This is also good on hamburgers (instead of other condiments) or on toasted or grilled bread.

Cost per serving (3½ T.): 47¢

NUTRITIONAL ANALYSIS PER SERVING
Calories: 195
Fat: 16 grams
Cholesterol: 48 mg
Carbohydrates: 7 grams
Fiber: 1 gram
Protein: 7 grams
Sodium: 251 mg

Kitchen Tip

FRESH HERBS are more flavorful than dried herbs and should be used whenever possible. But if you have only dried herbs, and a recipe calls for fresh, substitute using these amounts as a guide: 1 teaspoon dried=3 teaspoons fresh. Certain recipes, such as pesto, should not have a dried herb used in place of the fresh version.

Spiced Nuts

Serves 12
Preparation Time: 10 minutes

- 1 cup + 2 T. sugar
- 2 tsp. red pepper flakes
- 1 T. cayenne pepper
- 1 T. salt
- 6 T. peanut oil
- 4 cups peanuts, roasted (cashews work well also)

In a small bowl combine the 2 tablespoons sugar, red pepper flakes, cayenne pepper, and salt. Set aside.

In a skillet, heat the oil on medium heat. Add the peanuts and 1 cup of sugar. Stirring constantly, heat the mixture until the sugar has glazed around the nuts (about 2 to 3 minutes). Remove from heat and immediately shake the spices over the nuts and mix well.

Serve immediately. These can be stored in an airtight container but are best warm and fresh.

Cost per serving (⅓ cup): 46¢

NUTRITIONAL ANALYSIS PER SERVING
Calories: 410
Fat: 31 grams
Cholesterol: 0 mg
Carbohydrates: 27 grams
Fiber: 4 grams
Protein: 13 grams
Sodium: 542 mg

RED PEPPER FLAKES are made from dried and flaked chili peppers. Chili peppers come in a variety of colors, including red, orange, yellow, and green. Ground red pepper flakes are also known as cayenne pepper. Chili powder is cayenne pepper blended with other spices (cumin, garlic, marjoram, etc.).

Chinese Drumsticks

Serves 12
Preparation Time: 20 minutes
Cooking Time: 60 minutes

- 4 lbs. chicken drumsticks
- 1 T. soy sauce
- 1 clove garlic, pressed
- 4 egg whites
- 1 T. water
- 1 cup flour
- 1 cup homemade bread crumbs (see page 210)
- ½ tsp. pepper
- ½ tsp. ginger powder
- ½ cup sesame seeds

NUTRITIONAL ANALYSIS PER SERVING
Calories: 281
Fat: 13 grams
Cholesterol: 83 mg
Carbohydrates: 15 grams
Fiber: 1 gram
Protein: 24 grams
Sodium: 208 mg

Remove the skin from the drumsticks by pulling the skin back toward the joint and cutting off the skin.

In a shallow dish, combine soy sauce, garlic, egg whites, and water. Place the flour in another shallow dish. In a third shallow dish combine the bread crumbs, pepper, ginger, and sesame seeds.

Roll the drumsticks in the flour, then in the egg mix, then in the sesame seed mix. Place on a baking sheet. Bake at 350° for 60 minutes, or until cooked thoroughly.

Serve with a dipping sauce (sweet and sour, hoisin, plum sauce, etc.).

Cost per serving (2 drumsticks): 34¢

Chinese Drumsticks

(continued)

Kitchen Tip

SESAME SEEDS are harvested from the sesame plant, which is native to India, China, Indonesia, and Africa. Sesame oil is great for skin since it absorbs much of the ultraviolet rays of the sun and is water resistant. The seeds can be ground into a paste (tahini) that is used in cooking. Sesame seeds contain a high percentage of oil and therefore can go rancid. They should be stored for no more than 3 months in the cupboard, 6 months in the refrigerator, or 1 year in the freezer.

Salsa

Serves 8
Preparation Time: 10 minutes

- 5 cloves garlic
- ½ medium onion, quartered
- 1 cup fresh cilantro leaves, packed
- 28-oz. can stewed tomatoes
- 1 to 3 tsp. hot sauce (see page 204)
- 1 tsp. salt
- 1 tsp. lime or lemon juice

Put the garlic, onion, cilantro, and a third of the canned tomatoes in a blender. Cover and blend on medium power until the onion is in small (¼-inch) pieces. Add the rest of the ingredients to the blender and pulse 2 to 3 times or until the tomato is in small (¼-inch) pieces.

Cool and refrigerate in a tightly covered container. Salsa lasts 1 to 2 weeks in the refrigerator or up to 6 months in the freezer.

Serve with tortilla chips or as a sauce on salad.

Option: To increase the hotness of the salsa, add cayenne pepper (a dash at a time) or hot sauce (a few drops at a time) until you reach your desired strength. Also, a jalapeño pepper can be diced and added to the mix before you blend it.

Cost per serving (¼ cup): 38¢

NUTRITIONAL ANALYSIS PER SERVING
Calories: 30
Fat: 0 grams
Cholesterol: 0 mg
Carbohydrates: 6 grams
Fiber: 1 gram
Protein: 2 grams
Sodium: 478 mg

Kitchen Tip

SALSA is a general term meaning "sauce." Anything can be added to it, as the chef desires. Add diced vegetables (corn, bell peppers, green chilies, beans, etc.), and more or less hot sauce, and blend in a mixer (or don't blend) to achieve any desired consistency.

CHAPTER 3

Beverages

Cool Ade Slush

Serves 6
Preparation Time: 10 minutes

- 1 cup hot water
- 1 cup sugar
- .15-oz. packet unsweetened flavored drink mix
- 8 cups ice

Put the hot water, sugar, and the mix in a blender. Cover and blend for a few seconds until the sugar is dissolved. Add the ice and blend until the drink has a slushy texture. Serve immediately.

Cost per serving (1 cup): 6¢

NUTRITIONAL ANALYSIS PER SERVING	
Calories: 129	
Fat: 0 grams	
Cholesterol: 0 mg	
Carbohydrates: 33 grams	
Fiber: 0 grams	
Protein: 0 grams	
Sodium: 11 mg	

Kitchen Tip

The suffix ADE is used for beverages made with sugar, water, and fruit flavoring. Some common "ades" are lemonade, limeade, and orangeade.

Non-Alcoholic Fruit Daiquiri

Serves 1
Preparation Time: 5 minutes

- 3 oz. frozen fruit in syrup
- 1 tsp. sugar
- 1 oz. lime juice
- ½ cup ice

Place all of the ingredients in a blender. Cover and blend until smooth.

Garnish with a slice of orange or strawberry if desired. Serve immediately.

For a fancy touch, top with whipped cream before serving.

Cost per serving (¾ cup): 46¢

NUTRITIONAL ANALYSIS PER SERVING
Calories: 90
Fat: 0 grams
Cholesterol: 0 mg
Carbohydrates: 25 grams
Fiber: 2 grams
Protein: 1 gram
Sodium: 1 mg

 Kitchen Tip

Did you run out of SUGAR? You can substitute brown sugar for white sugar. Don't have that either? Use honey, corn syrup, or maple syrup. You can substitute an equal amount of these for sugar in liquid recipes, like the one above. Honey and maple syrup will change the flavor of a recipe slightly. When you use honey instead of sugar in a baking recipe, reduce the amount of liquid called for in the recipe (milk, water, etc.) by ¼ of the amount of honey used. For example, if you used 1 cup of honey instead of 1 cup of sugar, reduce the liquid called for in the recipe by ¼ cup; if you used ½ cup honey instead of ½ cup sugar, reduce the amount of liquid called for by 2 tablespoons (⅛ cup).

Wassail

Serves 16
Preparation Time: 5 minutes
Cooking Time: 10 to 15 minutes

- 2 qt. apple juice
- 2 cups orange juice
- 2 cups pineapple juice
- ¾ cup lemon juice
- 1 tsp. whole allspice

Place all of the ingredients in a large saucepan. Cover and heat over low heat until very warm, but do not boil.

Pour into an insulated pitcher or a punch bowl, straining the spices out as you pour. If serving in a punch bowl, garnish with a slice of orange or fresh apple slices.

Serve immediately.

Cost per serving (¾ cup): 20¢

NUTRITIONAL ANALYSIS PER SERVING
Calories: 93
Fat: 0 grams
Cholesterol: 0 mg
Carbohydrates: 23 grams
Fiber: 0 grams
Protein: 1 gram
Sodium: 4 mg

Kitchen Tip

To avoid having to STRAIN OUT SPICES from beverages, place the spices in a piece of cheesecloth and tie it closed. Let the spices steep, then remove the bag and discard.

Zesty Tomato Juice

Serves 1
Preparation Time: 5 minutes

- ½ cup tomato juice
- 1 T. lemon juice
- ½ tsp. Worcestershire sauce
- 1 dash hot sauce, or to taste (recipe on page 204)
- 1 pinch celery salt, or to taste
- 1 pinch salt, or to taste
- 1 pinch pepper, or to taste
- 1 dash lime juice, or to taste
- cracked ice (optional)

Combine all of the ingredients in a large glass. Stir well. Let sit for a minute to chill.

Pour off the liquid, leaving the ice behind (if desired).

For a nice presentation, serve with a stalk of celery as a garnish.

Cost per serving (½ cup): 38¢

NUTRITIONAL ANALYSIS PER SERVING	
Calories: 25	
Fat: 0 grams	
Cholesterol: 0 mg	
Carbohydrates: 7 grams	
Fiber: 1 gram	
Protein: 1 gram	
Sodium: 669 mg	

Kitchen Tip

If your CELERY STALKS have gotten limp, cover them in ice water and let them sit in the refrigerator overnight. They will be firmer the next day.

Coffee-Flavored Syrup

(like non-alcoholic Kahlúa)

Serves 26
Preparation Time: 5 minutes
Cooking Time: 5 minutes

- 2 cups water
- 3 cups sugar
- 3 T. instant coffee (don't use freeze-dried)
- 1 T. vanilla extract

Bring water, sugar, and coffee to a boil over medium heat. Turn the heat to low and simmer the sauce until the mixture becomes a thick syrup (about 2 to 5 minutes). Do not let it burn.

Let the syrup cool, and then add vanilla. Store in an airtight container in the refrigerator. It will keep for several weeks.

Use as a syrup over ice cream, add 2 tablespoons to a cup of coffee (iced or hot), or add 3 tablespoons to a glass of milk.

Cost per serving (2 T.): 3¢

NUTRITIONAL ANALYSIS PER SERVING
Calories: 90
Fat: 0 grams
Cholesterol: 0 mg
Carbohydrates: 23 grams
Fiber: 0 grams
Protein: 0 grams
Sodium: 1 mg

Kitchen Tip

To avoid watered-down drinks caused by melting ice cubes, make FLAVORED ICE CUBES out of the beverages that you drink most often (fruit juice, iced tea, coffee, lemonade, Kool-Aid, or even "flat" soda), and use them in place of regular ice cubes. If you prefer to drink water, liven up the water with unsweetened flavored ice cubes. Make these by adding a few drops of flavoring or extract (strawberry, orange, mint, etc.) to the water before freezing. Make the ice festive by adding sprigs of mint, orange or lemon peel, or a cherry.

Chocolate Raspberry Frosty

Serves 4
Preparation Time: 5 minutes

- 1 cup low-fat milk
- ½ cup chocolate syrup (see page 248)
- 3 cups frozen raspberries

Pour the milk and chocolate syrup into a blender. Add 1 cup of the raspberries, cover, and blend for 15 to 30 seconds. Repeat for the second and third cups of raspberries. Do not over mix, as this will thin the drink down.

Serve immediately.

Options: Substitute strawberries, bananas, or other frozen fruit for the raspberries.

Cost per serving (1 cup): 72¢

NUTRITIONAL ANALYSIS PER SERVING

Calories: 371	
Fat: 14 grams	
Cholesterol: 53 mg	
Carbohydrates: 58 grams	
Fiber: 0 grams	
Protein: 7 grams	
Sodium: 200 mg	

Kitchen Tip

For a quick and soothing BED-TIME DRINK, warm a glass of milk, add ¼ teaspoon of vanilla and ½ teaspoon of honey, mix, and enjoy! A dash of nutmeg or cinnamon adds even more flavor.

Flavored Iced Teas

Serves 8
Preparation Time: 5 minutes

- 2 qt. water
- 3 tea bags (individual serving size)
- flavorings (see list below)

Instead of buying bottled or canned flavored iced teas, make your own for a fraction of the cost. Any flavor tea can be made from a base of iced tea. To make the base, boil the water and remove from the heat. Pour the water over the tea bags and let them sit for 5 minutes. Do not use an aluminum container for brewing the tea, as the tea will take on a bad flavor.

For the flavorings, add any of the following to 2 quarts of brewed tea, and then chill after mixing:

- For lemon iced tea: ¾ cup sugar and ⅓ cup lemon juice
- For orange iced tea: ¾ cup sugar, ⅓ cup lemon juice, and ⅛ tsp. orange extract
- For strawberry iced tea: ¾ cup sugar, ⅓ cup lemon juice, and 1 T. strawberry extract
- For cranberry iced tea: ¾ cup sugar, ⅓ cup lemon juice, and 2 T. cranberry juice cocktail concentrate
- For mango iced tea: 1 cup mango juice
- For ginger-pineapple tea: 2 T. freshly grated gingerroot and 1½ cups pineapple juice

NOTE: I like my iced tea weak, so if the recipe tastes light to you, use 4 or 5 tea bags.

Cost per serving (1 cup): 16¢

NUTRITIONAL ANALYSIS PER SERVING
Calories: 80
Fat: 0 grams
Cholesterol: 0 mg
Carbohydrates: 21 grams
Fiber: 0 grams
Protein: 0 grams
Sodium: 1 mg

Flavored Iced Teas
(continued)

Kitchen Tip

There are two main TYPES OF TEAS: black and green. Both come from the same tea leaves, the difference being that black tea leaves are fermented before being dried. All varieties of tea come from the same evergreen shrub, but they are grown in different climates, creating variations in flavor. Both black and green teas contain antioxidants, but green tea contains more. Instant tea is made from granulated tea leaves. Herb tea is made from flowers, herbs, and spices and contains no black tea leaves.

Russian Tea Mix

Serves 39
Preparation Time: 15 minutes

- 1 cup Tang or other orange-flavored drink mix
- 1 cup sugar
- ¼ cup instant tea
- 3 T. sweetened lemonade mix
- ¼ tsp. ground cloves
- ¼ tsp. ground cinnamon

Mix all of these ingredients well. Store in an airtight glass or plastic container.

To make hot Russian tea, add 1 tablespoon of the mix to 1 cup of hot water. Stir well.

For iced Russian tea, add 1 tablespoon of the mix to 1 cup of cold water. Stir well, and add ice.

Garnish either drink with a slice of orange or lemon, and/or a stick of cinnamon.

Cost per serving (1 T.): 6¢

NUTRITIONAL ANALYSIS PER SERVING	
Calories: 40	
Fat: 0 grams	
Cholesterol: 0 mg	
Carbohydrates: 10 grams	
Fiber: 0 grams	
Protein: 0 grams	
Sodium: 1 mg	

Kitchen Tip

If you need a LARGE BATCH OF ICE, make larger ice cubes by freezing water in muffin trays. Once the ice is frozen, remove from the tins and store in plastic bags in the freezer.

Party Slush

Serves 28
Preparation Time: 10 minutes
Freezing Time: 24 hours

- 4 green-tea bags
- 9 cups boiling water
- 2 cups sugar
- 12 oz. frozen concentrated orange juice
- 12 oz. frozen concentrated pineapple juice
- 2 2-liter bottles lemon-lime soda or ginger ale

Place the tea bags in the boiling water. Add the sugar and stir until the sugar is dissolved. Steep for 5 minutes. Add the frozen juices and stir until well mixed. Freeze for 24 hours, stirring every 8 hours. This mixture will last for months in the freezer if stored in an airtight container.

To serve, put ½ cup of the slush mixture into a tall glass and fill the glass with lemon-lime soda or ginger ale.

Garnish drink with a slice of orange or pineapple.

Cost per serving (1 cup): 16¢

NUTRITIONAL ANALYSIS PER SERVING

Calories: 95

Fat: 0 grams

Cholesterol: 0 mg

Carbohydrates: 24 grams

Fiber: 0 grams

Protein: 1 gram

Sodium: 1 mg

Kitchen Tip

STEEPING is the act of soaking an element, such as tea bags, coffee grounds, herbs, or spices, in a hot liquid to infuse the flavor into the liquid.

V-5 Vegetable Juice

Serves 6
Preparation Time: 15 minutes

Many canned vegetable juices are made from overripe and even rotting vegetables.
Make your own fresh vegetable juice with healthy, even organic, vegetables.

- 6 fresh tomatoes
- 4 green onions
- ½ cup fresh parsley
- ¼ green bell pepper
- 1 celery stalk
- 1 tsp. salt
- 2 tsp. sugar
- ⅛ tsp. pepper
- ½ tsp. Worcestershire sauce
- 1 dash hot sauce (see page 204)

NUTRITIONAL ANALYSIS PER SERVING
Calories: 90
Fat: 1 gram
Cholesterol: 0 mg
Carbohydrates: 19 grams
Fiber: 5 grams
Protein: 5 grams
Sodium: 436 mg

Place all of the ingredients in a blender. Cover and blend on high until the mixture is smooth. Pour into glasses, straining first to catch peels and pulp. Serve immediately.

If the drink is too thick, dilute it with a small amount of water until it is the thickness that you like.

Garnish drink with a rib of celery if desired.

Cost per serving (1 cup): 56¢

Kitchen Tip

To SOFTEN FRESH VEGETABLES, boil in water for 2 to 3 minutes.

Coffeeccino

Serves 4
Preparation Time: 5 minutes

- 1½ cups cold coffee (decaf or regular)
- ½ cup milk
- ½ cup sugar
- 1 tsp. chocolate syrup (see page 248)
- ¼ tsp. vanilla
- 3 cups ice cubes

Place all of the ingredients in a blender. Cover and blend on high speed until the ice is crushed and the mixture is smooth. Pour into tall glasses and enjoy!

Variations: Add 2 T. caramel ice cream topping to the drink before blending, and/or top with whipped cream before serving.

Cost per serving (1⅓ cups): 11¢

NUTRITIONAL ANALYSIS PER SERVING
Calories: 115
Fat: 0 grams
Cholesterol: 1 mg
Carbohydrates: 28 grams
Fiber: 0 grams
Protein: 1 gram
Sodium: 25 mg

Kitchen Tip

If you make EXTRA COFFEE, don't throw it away: keep it for another recipe. You can refrigerate coffee in a covered jar for one month or freeze it for up to 6 months. Freeze it in a plastic container or in ice cube trays for easy use.

CHAPTER 4

Soups

Soups can make a healthy yet frugal meal that also warms the family, especially on a winter night. Additionally, soups are a great help to the budget. We keep a bowl in the freezer for leftover meats and vegetables and use them to make soup once a week. If there is a leg of chicken or some vegetables left in the pan, we put them in the bowl for a soup or stew. We accompany the soup with a homemade biscuit, like cheesy garlic biscuits (see page 171). These meals cost less than a dollar to serve all four of us. But frugality depends on how you shop for the ingredients and how much you pay for them.

Aside from being frugal, soups can provide all of the essential nutrients that you need from a meal: protein, vegetables, carbohydrates, fiber, etc. Look at the following recipes and see how loaded with nutrients they are. For example, the carrot soup has lots of vegetables and yields 10 grams of protein per serving. Other soups that are "meal worthy" (they contain vegetables, carbohydrates, and significant protein) are chicken noodle soup (15 grams of protein per serving) and hearty minestrone soup (14 grams of protein per serving), and hot and sour soup (10 grams of protein per serving). The protein can be increased by adding leftover meat or chicken. Soups can also be made ahead and frozen for busy evenings.

Hearty Minestrone Soup

Serves 8
Preparation Time: 20 minutes
Cooking Time: 40 minutes

- 1 T. olive oil
- ¾ cup diced onion
- 1 large carrot, thinly sliced
- 2 stalks celery, thinly sliced
- 2 cloves garlic, pressed
- 2 cups cubed zucchini
- 28-oz. can low-sodium stewed tomatoes
- 15-oz. can low-sodium chicken broth
- 1 cup water
- 1 tsp. Italian seasoning (see page 209)
- 14-oz. can sauerkraut, drained (it adds an awesome flavor to the soup)
- 15-oz. can garbanzo beans, drained
- 15-oz. can kidney beans, drained
- ¼ cup uncooked elbow macaroni
- ½ tsp. salt
- ¼ tsp. pepper

NUTRITIONAL ANALYSIS PER SERVING	
Calories: 228	
Fat: 4 grams	
Cholesterol: 0 mg	
Carbohydrates: 39 grams	
Fiber: 7 grams	
Protein: 14 grams	
Sodium: 676 mg	

Kitchen Tip

SAUTÉING VEGETABLES in oil or butter before adding the stock seals in their flavors. For onions it brings out their sweetness. And most soups improve their flavor when stored in the refrigerator for a day or two.

Heat the oil over medium heat in a large (6-qt.) pan. Add the onion, carrots, celery, and garlic. Sauté for 3 minutes, or until the garlic is light golden brown.

Add the zucchini, tomatoes, broth, water, Italian seasoning, and sauerkraut. Stir. Cover and simmer for 20 minutes.

Add the remaining ingredients, stir, cover, and simmer for 15 minutes, or until the macaroni is tender.

Note: This is excellent with some Parmesan cheese sprinkled on top.

Cost per serving (1½ cups): 79¢

Egg Drop Soup

Serves 4
Preparation Time: 5 minutes
Cooking Time: 15 minutes

- 4 cups water
- ⅓ cup broth powder (see page 226)
- 1 tsp. powdered ginger
- 2 eggs, beaten
- 1 green onion, sliced thinly

Heat water over medium heat in a large (2-qt.) pan. Add broth powder. Bring broth to a boil. Add the ginger and stir. While the broth is boiling, slowly drizzle the egg into the soup. Immediately remove from heat, stir in green onions, and serve.

Cost per serving (1½ cups): 12¢

NUTRITIONAL ANALYSIS PER SERVING	
Calories: 23	
Fat: 2 grams	
Cholesterol: 60 mg	
Carbohydrates: 1 gram	
Fiber: 0 grams	
Protein: 2 grams	
Sodium: 38 mg	

Kitchen Tip

This is a Chinese specialty, turning a simple cup of BROTH into a light meal. Add ingredients to taste (noodles, diced carrots, peas, etc.).

Jessica's Stone Soup

Serves 6
Preparation Time: 10 minutes
Cooking Time: 35 minutes

This is my daughter's favorite soup. She adapted it from the classic children's story.

- 2 T. oil
- ½ cup diced onion
- 2 cloves garlic, pressed
- ½ cup diced celery
- 1 cup diced carrot
- 10 cups water
- ⅓ cup broth powder (see page 226)
- 2 medium brown potatoes, peeled and diced
- salt and pepper to taste
- 1 small, nonporous washed stone (optional)

NUTRITIONAL ANALYSIS PER SERVING
Calories: 83
Fat: 5 grams
Cholesterol: 0 mg
Carbohydrates: 10 grams
Fiber: 2 grams
Protein: 1 gram
Sodium: 98 mg

Heat the oil over medium heat in a large (4-qt.) pan. Add onions, garlic, celery, and carrots. Sauté for 3 minutes or until garlic is light golden brown. Add the water, broth powder, potatoes, seasonings, and stone, if using. Bring the soup to a boil, then reduce heat to low and simmer for 30 minutes or until potatoes are tender. Remove from heat, discard the stone (if using), and serve.

Option: Add 1 cup diced cooked chicken (from your freezer bowl, to be thrifty) to the soup for a complete meal.

This is great served with cheesy garlic biscuits or easy refrigerator rolls (see pages 171 and 172).

Cost per serving (2 cups): 24¢

Kitchen Tip

When making broth from a turkey carcass or beef bone, freeze the EXTRA BROTH in ice cube trays, then when frozen, transfer the cubes to plastic bags. This allows for longer storage (6 months) and for easy use in soups and other recipes.

Tortilla Soup

Serves 6
Preparation Time: 15 minutes
Cooking Time: 30 minutes

- 1 lb. chicken breasts, cubed
- ½ cup finely diced onion
- 4 cloves garlic, pressed
- 6 cups water
- ⅓ cup broth powder (see page 226)
- 10-oz. can tomato sauce
- ¾ tsp. dry oregano
- ⅓ cup lime juice
- 1 tsp. chili powder
- 3.5-oz. bag tortilla chips

NUTRITIONAL ANALYSIS PER SERVING	
Calories: 295	
Fat: 14 grams	
Cholesterol: 34 mg	
Carbohydrates: 30 grams	
Fiber: 2 grams	
Protein: 15 grams	
Sodium: 951 mg	

In a large (4-qt.) pan, combine all of the ingredients (except the tortilla chips). Bring to a boil over medium heat. Reduce heat to low and simmer for 20 minutes or until the chicken is cooked thoroughly.

Serve with a handful of tortilla chips on the top of the soup.

Garnish with shredded Monterey Jack cheese, sliced avocado, or a teaspoon of sour cream in the center of each serving.

Cost per serving (1½ cups): 70¢

Kitchen Tip

TOMATO SAUCE is made by cooking tomatoes and straining the juice off, then blending the tomatoes into a sauce. TOMATO PASTE is tomato sauce that has been cooked for hours, evaporating the moisture to make a thick paste.

Quick Pea Soup

Serves 4
Preparation Time: 5 minutes
Cooking Time: 10 minutes

- 2 cups chicken stock (or water plus ⅓ cup broth powder; see page 226)
- 16-oz. can peas, drained
- ¼ tsp. onion powder
- ¼ tsp. pepper
- ¼ tsp. Italian seasoning (see page 209)
- ½ tsp. lemon juice

Combine all of the ingredients in a blender. Blend until smooth. Pour into a 2-quart saucepan. Heat over medium heat until hot. Serve immediately.

To add a yummy flare, add a teaspoon of sour cream or plain yogurt to the center of each bowl before serving.

Cost per serving (¾ cup): 23¢

NUTRITIONAL ANALYSIS PER SERVING	
Calories: 28	
Fat: 0 grams	
Cholesterol: 0 mg	
Carbohydrates: 4 grams	
Fiber: 3 grams	
Protein: 3 grams	
Sodium: 338 mg	

 Kitchen Tip

PEAS are a member of the legume family. The English pea is the common garden pea, meant to be eaten without the pod. Sugar snap peas and snow peas are eaten whole, pod and all. These are excellent raw or barely cooked, so their crisp texture is retained.

Chicken Noodle Soup

Serves 4
Preparation Time: 10 minutes
Cooking Time: 25 minutes

- ½ lb. boneless, skinless chicken breasts, diced
- 5 cups water
- 1 medium onion, diced
- 2 cloves garlic, pressed
- 1 cup diced carrot
- 1 cup diced celery
- 2 T. chopped fresh parsley
- ½ tsp. Italian seasoning (see page 209)
- ½ tsp. salt
- ½ tsp. pepper
- ½ cup wide egg noodles, uncooked

Place the chicken in a large (6-qt.) pan, and cover with the water. Add the onions, garlic, carrots, celery, parsley, Italian seasoning, salt, and pepper. Cover and heat to boiling over medium heat. Boil for 5 minutes. Add the noodles and simmer for 15 more minutes or until the chicken is cooked and the noodles and carrots are tender.

Cost per serving (1½ cups): 75¢

NUTRITIONAL ANALYSIS PER SERVING	
Calories: 123	
Fat: 1 gram	
Cholesterol: 37 mg	
Carbohydrates: 12 grams	
Fiber: 3 grams	
Protein: 15 grams	
Sodium: 503 mg	

 *Kitchen Tip*

Garlic cloves are not be confused with bulbs. The whole unit that grows under ground is called the BULB, made up of many sections called CLOVES. Garlic's strong flavor comes from the oils in the clove. An unbroken bulb can be stored in a cool dry place for up to 8 weeks. Once the bulb is broken into cloves, the cloves last 3 to 10 days.

Carrot Soup

Serves 4
Preparation Time: 15 minutes
Cooking Time: 35 minutes

- 2 T. butter
- ½ cup diced onion
- 2 cloves garlic, pressed
- 1½ cups water
- 1½ cups low-sodium chicken broth
- 2 cups peeled and chopped carrots
- 4 brown potatoes, peeled and chopped
- 1 tsp. sugar
- ½ tsp. salt
- ¼ tsp. pepper
- 1 cup buttermilk
- ½ tsp. ground ginger
- 1 tsp. horseradish
- 15-oz. can stewed tomatoes, diced

NUTRITIONAL ANALYSIS PER SERVING	
Calories: 206	
Fat: 7 grams	
Cholesterol: 19 mg	
Carbohydrates: 30 grams	
Fiber: 4 grams	
Protein: 10 grams	
Sodium: 800 mg	

 Kitchen Tip

"DRESS UP" SOUP for special occasions by serving it in tiny pumpkins that have been hollowed out or in small bread rounds that have the top third removed and the inside hollowed out.

In a large (4-qt.) pan, melt the butter over medium heat. Add onions and garlic. Sauté for 3 minutes or until the onion is soft and clear, stirring frequently. Add the water, broth, carrots, potatoes, sugar, salt, and pepper, and bring the soup to a boil. Reduce heat to low and simmer for 20 minutes or until the carrots and potatoes are tender.

Remove soup from heat and let it cool slightly. Pour into a blender or food processor. Add the buttermilk, ginger, and horseradish. Blend until creamy. Add the tomatoes. Blend for very short bursts (3 seconds each)—use the "pulse" feature on your

Carrot Soup

(continued)

blender if you have one—to blend the tomatoes in without removing the chunks of tomato completely.

If desired, garnish with a teaspoon of sour cream in the center of each soup bowl. This is great served with cheesy garlic biscuits (see page 171).

Note: The carrots can be replaced with an equal amount of pumpkin or butternut squash flesh.

Cost per serving (2 cups): 66¢

Mulligatawny Soup

Serves 4
Preparation Time: 15 minutes
Cooking Time: 30 minutes

Mulligatawny is a soup created by Indian chefs in the eighteenth century for the British ruling class in India. It has numerous versions, but this is close to the original, obtained from local chefs while we lived in Pakistan.

- 2 T. oil
- ½ cup diced onion
- 1 medium carrot, diced
- 2 stalks celery, diced
- 2 cloves garlic, pressed
- 4 tsp. flour
- 1 tsp. curry powder
- ⅛ tsp. Italian seasoning (see page 209)
- ¼ tsp. ground ginger
- ½ tsp. salt
- ¼ tsp. pepper
- ¼ cup broth powder (see page 226)
- 4 cups water
- ¼ cup diced tart green apple
- ½ cup buttermilk

NUTRITIONAL ANALYSIS PER SERVING

Calories:	105
Fat:	7 grams
Cholesterol:	1 mg
Carbohydrates:	8 grams
Fiber:	2 grams
Protein:	2 grams
Sodium:	419 mg

In a large (4-qt.) pan, heat the oil over medium heat. Add onions, carrots, celery, and garlic. Sauté for 3 minutes or until the onion is soft and clear, stirring frequently. Stir in the flour, curry powder, Italian seasoning, ginger, salt, and pepper to form a paste. Add the broth powder, water, and apple, and simmer for 10 minutes or until the carrots are tender. Remove soup from heat and let it cool slightly. Just before serving, stir in the buttermilk.

Options: Some recipes add ½ cup diced meat (of

Kitchen Tip

CREAM SOUPS usually contain a high-fat cream or a butter-based thickener. To avoid the fat and keep the thickening, add diced potato to the soup and puree the soup after cooking, or cook and puree the potato separately and then add to the soup.

Mulligatawny Soup

(continued)

any type), ¼ cup cooked rice, ⅓ cup cooked lentils, ¼ cup sliced mushrooms, and/or ½ tsp. coriander to suit individual tastes. These can be added at the same time as the apple.

Cost per serving (1½ cups): 35¢

Hot and Sour Soup

Serves 4
Preparation Time: 10 minutes
Cooking Time: 35 minutes

- 2 cups low-sodium chicken broth
- ½ cup thinly sliced mushrooms
- 1 tsp. minced ginger
- 2 T. thinly sliced bamboo shoots (optional)
- 1 T. cornstarch
- 1 T. low-sodium soy sauce
- 2 to 3 drops Tabasco sauce
- ½ cup firm tofu cut in ½-inch cubes (or substitute any diced meat)
- 1 egg, beaten
- ¼ tsp. pepper
- 3 T. red wine vinegar
- 1 green onion, thinly sliced

NUTRITIONAL ANALYSIS PER SERVING	
Calories: 70	
Fat: 2 grams	
Cholesterol: 45 mg	
Carbohydrates: 8 grams	
Fiber: 2 grams	
Protein: 10 grams	
Sodium: 402 mg	

In a large (4-qt.) pan, heat the broth over medium heat. Add the mushrooms, ginger, and bamboo shoots. Bring to a boil. In a small bowl, make a paste with the cornstarch, soy sauce, and the Tabasco. Add the paste to the soup and stir to mix in. Continue boiling and stirring until the soup reaches a thicker consistency. Add the tofu. Drizzle the egg slowly into the soup. Remove from heat. Let it cool for 1 to 2 minutes. Add the pepper, vinegar, and green onion and stir. Serve immediately.

Note: You can add other items to the soup to suit your taste such as ½ cup thinly sliced pork (pre-cooked), crabmeat, or other favorite meats. Use meats from your freezer bowl to be extra thrifty. You can use any variety mushrooms you prefer (shiitake, portobello, etc.). You can add ½ cup shredded bok choy (Chinese cabbage) also.

Cost per serving (1 cup): 68¢

Kitchen Tip

When a soup calls for CORN-STARCH, never add it directly to the hot soup. It will lump. Add it to a few teaspoons of cold liquid (such as the broth you are using or water) to form a thin paste, and then add it to the soup.

Vegetable Chowder

Serves 6
Preparation Time: 15 minutes
Cooking Time: 35 minutes

- 3 T. oil
- ½ cup diced onion
- 2 cloves garlic, pressed
- 2 stalks celery, diced
- ¼ cup flour
- ½ tsp. salt
- ¼ tsp. pepper
- ½ tsp. Italian seasoning (see page 209)
- 1½ cups peeled and diced potatoes
- 2 cups diced winter vegetables (parsnips, carrots, turnips, rutabagas)
- 4 cups water
- ¼ cup broth powder (see page 226)
- 2 cups low-fat milk

In a large (6-qt.) pan, heat the oil over medium heat. Add onions, garlic, and celery. Sauté for 3 minutes or until the onion is soft and clear, stirring frequently. Stir in the flour, salt, pepper, and Italian seasoning to form a paste. Add the potatoes, winter vegetables, water, and broth powder. Stir to blend the paste in—using a whisk works best. Simmer for 30 minutes or until the vegetables are tender. Remove soup from heat and let it cool slightly. Just before serving, stir in the milk.

Variation: To make clam chowder, omit the winter vegetables and add 1 cup canned clams in their place.

Note: This is a great recipe for using your freezer soup bowl contents. Use it in place of the winter vegetables.

Cost per serving (1½ cups): 28¢

NUTRITIONAL ANALYSIS PER SERVING

Calories: 140

Fat: 8 grams

Cholesterol: 3 mg

Carbohydrates: 14 grams

Fiber: 1 gram

Protein: 4 grams

Sodium: 293 mg

Kitchen Tip

It is an old wives' tale that if you accidentally add TOO MUCH SALT to a soup, you can add a few slices of raw potato to soak up some of the excess salt. In reality, all you can do is add more water and other ingredients to dilute the salt. To cook without salt, replace the salt with an equal amount of lemon juice.

Sweet Potato Soup

Serves 4
Preparation Time: 1 hour, 15 minutes
Cooking Time: 15 minutes

- 1 lb. sweet potato (about 2 medium potatoes)
- ¼ cup milk
- 2 T. butter
- ¼ tsp. ground ginger
- 1 tsp. salt
- dash pepper
- ⅛ tsp. Italian seasoning (see page 209)
- 4 cups water

Wash the sweet potatoes and bake at 375° for 45 minutes or until they are soft in the center. Remove from the oven and let cool. Once you can handle them, open them, scoop out the pulp, and place it in a large mixing bowl. Add milk, butter, ginger, salt, pepper, and Italian seasoning. Blend with a potato masher or with the mixer to make a mashed potato–like consistency.

In a large (4-qt.) pan, heat water over medium heat. Stir in the potato mix and bring to a boil. Reduce the heat and let simmer for 10 minutes.

If desired, serve with a tablespoon of sour cream in the center of each bowl.

Cost per serving (2 cups): 52¢

NUTRITIONAL ANALYSIS PER SERVING	
Calories: 155	
Fat: 6 grams	
Cholesterol: 17 mg	
Carbohydrates: 22 grams	
Fiber: 3 grams	
Protein: 3 grams	
Sodium: 691 mg	

Kitchen Tip

BUTTER comes in various forms: UNSALTED BUTTER is pure cream churned into butter without salt; SWEET BUTTER is another name for unsalted or lightly salted butter; SWEET CREAM BUTTER is usually just unsalted butter with a fancy name. Unless butter states that it is unsalted or sweet, it is salted. Store butter for up to 1 month in the refrigerator or for up to 6 months in the freezer. Store butter tightly wrapped since it absorbs flavors easily.

CHAPTER 5

Vegetables and Side Dishes

Carrot Salad

Serves 6
Preparation Time: 15 minutes
Chilling Time: overnight

- 2 cups grated carrots (about 4 medium)
- 8 oz. canned crushed pineapple, drained
- ½ cup raisins
- 8 oz. vanilla yogurt
- ½ tsp. nutmeg (or more to taste)

Mix all of the ingredients in a large mixing bowl. Cover and chill overnight in the refrigerator to enhance the flavor.

Variations: Try lemon or peach yogurt for a new taste combination.

Cost per serving (¾ cup): 44¢

NUTRITIONAL ANALYSIS PER SERVING	
Calories: 109	
Fat: 1 gram	
Cholesterol: 2 mg	
Carbohydrates: 24 grams	
Fiber: 3 grams	
Protein: 3 grams	
Sodium: 53 mg	

Kitchen Tip

GRATING reduces food into small pieces, making it easier to incorporate one food into another.

Zesty Low-fat Fries

Serves 8
Preparation Time: 15 minutes
Cooking Time: 35 minutes

- 6 brown potatoes
- ¼ cup vegetable oil
- 3 T. lemon juice
- 1 tsp. garlic powder
- 1 tsp. onion powder
- 1 T. Italian seasoning (see page 209)
- 1 tsp. salt
- ½ tsp. pepper
- ½ tsp. hot sauce (see page 204)

NUTRITIONAL ANALYSIS PER SERVING	
Calories: 115	
Fat: 7 grams	
Cholesterol: 0 mg	
Carbohydrates: 13 grams	
Fiber: 1 gram	
Protein: 2 grams	
Sodium: 271 mg	

Slice potatoes into ¼- to ½-inch strips, and place in a bowl. In another bowl, mix all the remaining ingredients. Pour over the potato strips and mix well.

Spread potatoes evenly in a single layer on a baking sheet. Bake at 450° for 35 minutes, or until tender and golden brown.

Note: To make the fries even crispier, soak the strips of raw potato in ice water for 30 minutes, then pat dry before combining with seasonings.

Cost per serving (1 cup): 22¢

Kitchen Tip

To STORE POTATOES for long periods, keep them in a cool, dark bin at 50° or less (but not in the refrigerator). Allow space between the potatoes so air can circulate around them well.

Stuffing

Serves 10
Preparation Time: 20 minutes
Cooking Time: 25 minutes
Recipe donated by Joan Stivers

- ½ cup butter, melted
- 1 cup chopped celery
- 1 onion, chopped
- ½ tsp. salt
- 1 tsp. pepper
- ¼ cup chopped parsley
- 1 tsp. powdered sage
- 1 tsp. powdered thyme
- 1 tsp. powdered oregano
- 4 cups bread cubes (see Kitchen Tip below)

NUTRITIONAL ANALYSIS PER SERVING	
Calories: 343	
Fat: 13 grams	
Cholesterol: 25 mg	
Carbohydrates: 49 grams	
Fiber: 3 grams	
Protein: 9 grams	
Sodium: 228 mg	

Melt the butter in a large skillet. Add the celery, onions, salt, and pepper. Cook until the onions are clear (1 to 2 minutes). Transfer to a large mixing bowl. Add the parsley and seasonings and mix in. Add the bread, and toss well to coat the bread with the seasoning. Stuff into turkey or chicken cavity and bake according to poultry directions.

If baking in a dish—not in a bird—place in a deep dish, pour 3 cups broth or water over the stuffing, and cover with a lid or with foil. Bake at 350° for 25 minutes.

Variations: Add 1 cup of any of the following for extra flavor: cranberries, nuts (walnuts, pine nuts, pecans, or Brazil nuts), mushrooms, oysters, cooked sausage, cooked wild rice, water chestnuts, or clams. Add these while tossing the bread with the seasonings.

Cost per serving (⅔ cup): 28¢

Kitchen Tip

To MAKE BREAD CUBES for stuffing, lay slices of bread (stale bread is fine) in a single layer on an oven rack. Bake at 250˚ for 1 to 3 minutes, until golden brown. Watch closely so they don't burn. Once cooled, break apart into small pieces with your fingers.

Glazed Carrots

Serves 5
Preparation Time: 5 minutes
Cooking Time: 10 minutes

- 1 lb. baby carrots
- ¼ tsp. salt
- 3 cups water
- 1 T. butter
- 1 T. maple syrup (or honey)
- ⅛ tsp. powdered ginger

In a large saucepan, combine the carrots, salt, and water. Boil the carrots over medium heat for 5 minutes. Pour carrots into a colander and let drain until the sauce is ready.

In the same empty saucepan over medium heat, heat the butter, maple syrup, and ginger. Do not burn this mixture. Add the carrots to the pan, and gently toss them until well coated with the glaze. Turn onto a serving platter and drizzle the remaining glaze over the carrots.

Cost per serving (½ cup): 37¢

NUTRITIONAL ANALYSIS PER SERVING
Calories: 68
Fat: 2 grams
Cholesterol: 6 mg
Carbohydrates: 12 grams
Fiber: 2 grams
Protein: 1 gram
Sodium: 214 mg

Kitchen Tip

BABY CARROTS are young carrots that are picked before they grow large. They offer a sweeter flavor than a full-grown carrot. Most of the carrots sold as "baby carrots" in stores today are actually large carrots that have been cut and shaped to look like baby carrots.

Fried Rice

Serves 6
Preparation Time: 10 minutes
Cooking Time: 10 minutes

- 2 T. oil
- ¾ cup diced onion
- 2 cloves garlic, pressed
- 4 egg whites
- 2½ cups cooked rice
- 1 cup frozen peas and carrots, thawed
- ½ tsp. ground ginger
- 2 T. low-sodium soy sauce
- 2 green onions, thinly sliced

NUTRITIONAL ANALYSIS PER SERVING	
Calories: 169	
Fat: 4 grams	
Cholesterol: 0 mg	
Carbohydrates: 27 grams	
Fiber: 2 grams	
Protein: 6 grams	
Sodium: 257 mg	

In a skillet, heat the oil over medium heat. Add the onions and garlic; stir and cook for 1 to 2 minutes. Add the egg whites and cook while constantly stirring. Remove eggs, garlic, and onions, and put on plate. Add rice to the pan and cook for 2 to 3 minutes while stirring constantly. Add the peas and carrots, ginger, and soy sauce. Stir while cooking for an additional 2 minutes. Remove from heat. Return the eggs to the pan, add the green onions, and mix well.

This is great with broccoli beef (see page 104).

Note: This can be turned into a meal by adding 1 cup diced cooked meat with the peas and carrots. It's a great way to use up leftover meat.

Cost per serving (¾ cup): 28¢

Kitchen Tip

To make your preparation time go faster, chop several ONIONS at one time. Store in the freezer in an airtight container or sealed plastic bag for up to 4 months. Take out what you need and return the rest to the freezer.

Fruit Salad

Serves 6
Preparation Time: 10 minutes

- 8 oz. lemon-flavored yogurt
- ¼ tsp. vanilla extract
- ½ tsp. nutmeg
- 8-oz. can mandarin oranges, drained
- 2 green apples, diced (not peeled)
- 2 bananas, sliced

In a large mixing bowl combine the yogurt with the vanilla and nutmeg. Add the fruit and toss.

Serve immediately.

Note: If there are leftovers, put the salad in a blender and make a smoothie.

Cost per serving (1 cup): 43¢

NUTRITIONAL ANALYSIS PER SERVING	
Calories: 80	
Fat: 2 grams	
Cholesterol: 5 mg	
Carbohydrates: 16 grams	
Fiber: 2 grams	
Protein: 2 grams	
Sodium: 19 mg	

Kitchen Tip

NUTMEG is a hard seed from the nutmeg tree, which is an evergreen. The walnut-sized seed is dried and ground to be used as a spice. If you grate your own nutmeg, the flavor and aroma will be remarkably better than the pre-grated version. The spice MACE is made from the membrane that surrounds the nutmeg nut before it is dried. The membrane is dried and ground to make mace.

Spanish Rice

Serves 4
Preparation Time: 10 minutes
Cooking Time: 5 minutes

- 1 cup cooked rice
- ½ cup diced onion
- 1 clove garlic, pressed
- 15-oz. can diced Mexican-style tomatoes, or 2 cups salsa (see page 34), or 2 cups diced tomatoes plus 2 T. diced canned green chilies
- ½ tsp. salt
- 2 tsp. chili powder

Combine all of the ingredients in a medium saucepan. Stir over medium heat until bubbling. Remove from heat and serve.

Cost per serving (¾ cup): 35¢

NUTRITIONAL ANALYSIS PER SERVING
Calories: 96
Fat: 1 gram
Cholesterol: 0 mg
Carbohydrates: 21 grams
Fiber: 2 grams
Protein: 3 grams
Sodium: 522 mg

Kitchen Tip

CHILI POWDER is cayenne pepper (ground red pepper flakes) blended with other spices such as cumin, garlic powder, onion powder, marjoram, oregano, cloves, and coriander.

Pasta Salad

Serves 10
Cooking Time: 15 minutes
Preparation Time: 15 minutes

- 12 oz. pasta spirals
- 3 T. oil
- ¼ cup red wine vinegar
- 2 cloves garlic, pressed
- ½ tsp. salt
- ½ tsp. pepper
- ½ tsp. Italian seasoning (see page 209)
- 1 cup chopped broccoli
- 1 cup diced carrots
- ½ cup diced celery
- ½ cup diced red onion
- 1 red bell pepper, diced

Cook the pasta according to package directions. Run under cold water until pasta is cool.

In a large salad bowl mix the oil, vinegar, garlic, salt, pepper, and Italian seasoning. Add the pasta and vegetables, and toss until dressing is evenly distributed. The flavor improves the second day if covered and stored in the refrigerator.

Option: Add ½ cup grated Parmesan cheese to the vegetables while tossing.

Cost per serving (1 cup): 38¢

NUTRITIONAL ANALYSIS PER SERVING
Calories: 172
Fat: 5 grams
Cholesterol: 0 mg
Carbohydrates: 28 grams
Fiber: 2 grams
Protein: 5 grams
Sodium: 143 mg

Kitchen Tip

PASTA comes in over 600 shapes and sizes, all made from the same recipe. If pasta is going to be eaten right away, rinsing it is not necessary after draining. If the pasta will rest for 15 minutes or longer, rinse with warm water so it doesn't get pasty. The best way to reheat pasta without drying it out is to pour boiling water over it as it sits in a colander or to microwave it.

Winter Greens

Serves 4
Preparation Time: 10 minutes
Cooking Time: 5 minutes

Research has shown that women who consume at least six servings (½ cup each) of dark green leafy vegetables per week have half the risk of ovarian cancer as compared to those who consume only two servings per week.

- 1 lb. winter greens (kale, Swiss chard, mustard greens, collards, or spinach)
- 3 T. oil
- ¼ cup diced onion
- 1 clove garlic, pressed
- ¾ tsp. salt
- 2 T. Parmesan cheese
- 2 tsp. lemon juice or balsamic vinegar
- ½ cup homemade bread crumbs (see page 210)

NUTRITIONAL ANALYSIS PER SERVING	
Calories: 178	
Fat: 12 grams	
Cholesterol: 2 mg	
Carbohydrates: 15 grams	
Fiber: 3 grams	
Protein: 4 grams	
Sodium: 553 mg	

Wash the greens, drain well, and pat dry with a paper towel. Cut greens into 1-inch sections, and throw away the stems.

Heat the oil over medium heat in a large skillet. Add onions and garlic and cook, while stirring, for 1 to 2 minutes or until garlic is golden. Add greens and sprinkle with salt. Toss while cooking for 1 minute or until the greens barely begin to wilt. Do not cook until they are limp. (If your pan cannot hold all of the greens, cook them in batches.) Place the cooked greens in a large mixing bowl, and toss with the cheese, lemon juice, and bread crumbs. Serve immediately.

Note: Crumbled bacon (3 T.) is a tasty addition to this dish.

Cost per serving (1 cup): 49¢

 *Kitchen Tip*

Different greens have different tastes and textures. KALE has a mild flavor. SWISS CHARD has a bitter and salty flavor. MUSTARD GREENS have a mustard-like flavor. COLLARDS are from the cabbage family and have a bitter taste. Greens shouldn't be stored wet to avoid wilting.

Corn Soufflé

Serves 4
Preparation Time: 5 minutes
Cooking Time: 50 minutes

- 10 oz. frozen corn, thawed
- 2 T. diced onion
- ½ tsp. hot sauce (see page 204)
- 3 eggs
- ½ tsp. salt
- 1 cup milk

Put all of the ingredients in a blender and blend on medium setting until the mix is creamy (about 15 seconds).

Pour into a greased 8x8 pan. Bake at 350° for 50 minutes, or until it is set and no longer runny in the center.

Cost per serving (1 cup): 37¢

NUTRITIONAL ANALYSIS PER SERVING	
Calories: 135	
Fat: 5 grams	
Cholesterol: 138 mg	
Carbohydrates: 17 grams	
Fiber: 2 grams	
Protein: 8 grams	
Sodium: 367 mg	

Kitchen Tip

To THAW FROZEN FRUITS OR VEGETABLES, place them in a colander and run warm water over them.

Honey-Dijon Vegetables

Serves 8
Preparation Time: 10 minutes
Cooking Time: 10 minutes

- 1½ cups water
- 1½ cups carrots cut into ½-inch slices
- 1½ cups cauliflower cut into 1½-inch sections
- 1½ cups broccoli cut into 1½-inch sections
- 2 T. butter
- 2 T. diced onion
- 2 T. white flour
- 1 cup low-fat milk
- 1½ T. Dijon mustard
- 1 T. honey
- ½ tsp. broth powder (see page 226)

NUTRITIONAL ANALYSIS PER SERVING
Calories: 67
Fat: 3 grams
Cholesterol: 9 mg
Carbohydrates: 8 grams
Fiber: 1 gram
Protein: 2 grams
Sodium: 100 mg

In a medium saucepan, bring the water, carrots, cauliflower, and broccoli to a boil. Let boil, covered, for 5 minutes, or until the vegetables are at the desired tenderness. Drain and set aside.

Melt butter in a large skillet. Add the onion and cook until the onion is transparent but not brown. Add the flour and mix into a paste. Stir in the milk and mix well (using a whisk is best). Cook over medium heat for 1 to 2 minutes, stirring constantly, until thickened. Add the mustard, honey, and broth powder. Stir to mix. Add the vegetables, and stir.

Variation: This sauce is delicious over baked chicken and baked potatoes.

Cost per serving (¾ cup): 38¢

Kitchen Tip

When boiling CAULIFLOWER, it sometimes becomes an off-white color. To keep it snow-white, add 1 tablespoon of white distilled vinegar or lemon juice to the water as it boils.

Oven-Roasted Vegetables

Serves 6
Preparation Time: 15 minutes
Cooking Time: 45 minutes

- 10 small red new potatoes, 1 or 2 inches in diameter
- ¼ cup olive oil
- 3 T. lemon juice
- 3 cloves garlic, pressed
- 1 tsp. dried rosemary
- 1 tsp. dried oregano
- 1 tsp. salt
- ½ tsp. pepper
- 1 cup carrots sliced ½-inch thick
- 1 onion, chopped
- 2 red bell peppers, diced

NUTRITIONAL ANALYSIS PER SERVING
Calories: 222
Fat: 9 grams
Cholesterol: 0 mg
Carbohydrates: 33 grams
Fiber: 4 grams
Protein: 4 grams
Sodium: 468 mg

Wash each potato and cut into four pieces. Each piece should be between ½- and ¾-inch wide.

In a large mixing bowl, mix the oil, lemon juice, garlic, rosemary, oregano, salt, and pepper. Add the vegetables, and toss to distribute the sauce evenly.

Place vegetable mixture on a rimmed cooking sheet and spread to evenly distribute on the pan. Bake at 450° for 30 minutes, uncovered. Stir the vegetables a bit. Cook for an additional 15 minutes. Serve immediately.

Cost per serving (¾ cup): 69¢

Kitchen Tip

NEW POTATOES are simply young potatoes. They are desired in cooking because they are sweeter and crisper than a fully grown potato. The starch has not had time to develop and makes a firmer texture than a full-grown potato. They are used in recipes like the one above because they can hold their shape while being cooked and stirred and will still be firm when fully cooked.

Polenta

Serves 6
Preparation Time: 5 minutes
Cooking Time: 10 minutes

- 3 cups water
- 1 cup cornmeal
- ½ tsp. garlic powder
- ½ tsp. salt
- ½ tsp. Italian seasoning (see page 209)

NUTRITIONAL ANALYSIS PER SERVING
Calories: 86
Fat: 0 grams
Cholesterol: 0 mg
Carbohydrates: 18 grams
Fiber: 2 grams
Protein: 2 grams
Sodium: 3 mg

Combine all of the ingredients in a 2-quart sauce-pan. Bring to a boil over medium heat. Boil for 5 to 10 minutes, stirring frequently, until the cornmeal is tender. Pour into a greased 8x8 pan. You can serve this hot, or let cool in the refrigerator until set (2 hours).

If serving cold, cut into squares or cut with a cookie cutter into shapes. Store in an airtight container until needed. To use, reheat in the microwave oven.

Polenta tastes great in place of noodles: top with spaghetti sauce, pesto sauce, Alfredo sauce, or beef stew. Or eat it plain. Some people fry polenta in olive oil to crisp the outside.

Cost per serving (½ cup): 7¢

Kitchen Tip

POLENTA is a common side dish in Italy and has spread in popularity to many countries. Polenta is also called cornmeal mush in some cultures. It can be served hot, scooped out of the pan instead of shaped into squares. It is often served with melted butter on top. Often herbs or cheese are added to the polenta while cooking to add flavor; add up to ½ pound grated Parmesan, Romano, or Gorgonzola cheese to the polenta at the end of the cooking time.

Honey Mustard Salad

Serves 4
Preparation Time: 10 minutes

- ½ head romaine lettuce
- ¼ cup honey mustard dressing (see page 193)
- 3 green onions, thinly sliced
- ½ cup salted peanuts, chopped
- salt and pepper to taste

Rinse and drain the lettuce leaves. Tear into 1-inch pieces, and place the lettuce in a large mixing bowl. Pour the dressing evenly over the lettuce. Sprinkle with green onions, peanuts, and salt and pepper. Toss well. Serve immediately.

Variation: To make this a main dish, add 1 cup of cooked diced chicken to the salad.

Cost per serving (1½ cups): 28¢

NUTRITIONAL ANALYSIS PER SERVING
Calories: 142
Fat: 9 grams
Cholesterol: 3 mg
Carbohydrates: 14 grams
Fiber: 4 grams
Protein: 5 grams
Sodium: 153 mg

Kitchen Tip

There are numerous types of LETTUCE grown around the world. In the United States, there are four main types of lettuce: butter, crisp, leaf, and romaine. BUTTER lettuce is also known as butterhead, Boston, Bibb, and limestone lettuce. These have the mildest flavors and smoothest leaves, hence the name *butter*. CRISP lettuce is also known as iceberg lettuce. It has very crisp leaves and very little flavor. LEAF lettuce has straight leaves that stand up rather than curve to form a ball. Examples of leaf lettuce are red leaf lettuce and green leaf lettuce. The difference between leaf lettuce and ROMAINE is that romaine has a crisp and firm stalk that extends the length of each leaf, whereas the leaf lettuce stalk ends early in the leaf.

To easily REMOVE THE CORE of a head of lettuce, hit the core on the counter and it should loosen for easy removal. To store lettuce, wash (but do not soak) the leaves, pat dry or use a salad spinner to remove most of the moisture, and store in an airtight bag in the refrigerator for 3 to 5 days. As with winter greens, the darker the green color, the more nutrients in the lettuce.

Wheat Berry Salad

Serves 4
Preparation Time: 10 minutes
Cooking Time: 45 minutes

- ½ cup wheat berries

- 2 cups water

- 3 cups diced vegetables (broccoli, carrot, celery, bell pepper, zucchini, eggplant, leeks, etc.)

- 1 T. oil

- ½ cup diced onion

- 2 cloves garlic, pressed

- 15-oz. can diced tomatoes

- 1 tsp. lemon juice

- 2 tsp. Italian seasoning (see page 209)

- ½ tsp. salt

- ½ tsp. pepper

NUTRITIONAL ANALYSIS PER SERVING

Calories: 92	
Fat: 4 grams	
Cholesterol: 0 mg	
Carbohydrates: 15 grams	
Fiber: 6 grams	
Protein: 4 grams	
Sodium: 518 mg	

In a 2-qt. pan, heat the wheat berries and water over medium heat. Simmer covered for 40 minutes or until the berries are tender. While this is cooking, in a separate 2-qt. pan, cover the vegetables with water and bring to a boil. Boil for 3 to 4 minutes, then remove from heat and drain. They should still be a bit crisp.

In a large skillet, heat the oil over medium heat and sauté the onion and garlic for 3 to 4 minutes or until the onion is clear. Add the vegetables and continue stirring. Drain the berries and add them while stirring. Add the tomatoes, lemon juice, and seasonings, and stir while cooking for an additional 2 to 3 minutes. Serve immediately, or chill and serve cold.

Cost per serving (¾ cup): 68¢

Kitchen Tip

WHEAT BERRY is the term for the whole, unrefined wheat kernel. Wheat berries are high in protein and contain the healthy wheat germ. They can be purchased at health food stores. They are mainly used for grinding into flour and for baking bread, but can be boiled (as in this recipe) and eaten as a side dish or as a hot cereal. The term "cracked wheat" means the entire kernel is present but broken.

Marinated Vegetable Salad

Serves 6
Preparation Time: 15 minutes
Cooking Time: 10 minutes
Chilling Time: overnight

- 4 cups diced raw vegetables (carrots, broccoli, cauliflower, red bell pepper, jicama, zucchini, celery, etc.)
- ½ cup olive oil
- ¼ cup red wine vinegar
- ½ cup chopped onions
- 3 cloves garlic, pressed
- ½ tsp. Italian seasoning (see page 209)

Place the diced vegetables in a 2-qt. saucepan and cover with water. Cover the pan and bring to a boil over medium heat. Simmer for 5 to 10 minutes, or until the vegetables are still crisp but tender. Remove from heat, drain, and run under cold water.

Place the rest of the ingredients in a large mixing bowl and mix until well blended. Add the vegetables and toss. Cover and chill. Chill overnight in the refrigerator to enhance the flavor.

Variations: Add thin strips of cheese or salami, fresh parsley, black or green olives, or jalapeño peppers.

Cost per serving (¾ cup): 72¢

NUTRITIONAL ANALYSIS PER SERVING	
Calories: 171	
Fat: 18 grams	
Cholesterol: 0 mg	
Carbohydrates: 3 grams	
Fiber: 1 gram	
Protein: 1 gram	
Sodium: 55 mg	

Kitchen Tip

JICAMA is a large round root with a tough brown skin. It has a crunchy white meat with a slightly sweet and nutty flavor. It is excellent raw. To prepare, cut off the skin and slice the meat into sticks. Add it to a raw vegetable plate offered with dip. This will store well in the refrigerator for two weeks if kept sealed in a plastic bag.

Teriyaki Vegetables

Serves 6
Preparation Time: 10 minutes
Cooking Time: 10 minutes

- 3 cups diced raw vegetables (carrots, broccoli, cauliflower, red bell peppers, jicama, zucchini, celery, sliced water chestnuts, etc.)
- ¼ cup teriyaki sauce (see page 200)

Place the vegetables in a 2-qt. saucepan and cover with water. Cover the pan and bring to a boil over medium heat. Simmer for 5 to 10 minutes, or until the vegetables are still crisp but tender. Remove from heat and drain. Place in a large bowl and drizzle teriyaki sauce over the vegetables. Toss to distribute the sauce evenly.

Variation: Toss the vegetables and sauce with cooked pasta.

Cost per serving (½ cup): 18¢

NUTRITIONAL ANALYSIS PER SERVING

Calories: 32

Fat: 0 grams

Cholesterol: 0 mg

Carbohydrates: 8 grams

Fiber: 1 gram

Protein: 1 gram

Sodium: 92 mg

Kitchen Tip

To retain nutrients, COOK VEGETABLES and fruit as briefly as possible. The vitamin C and enzymes in vegetables and fruits are water-soluble and heat-sensitive. The water they are cooked in does not retain these lost elements.

CHAPTER 6

Main Dishes

Enchilada Meatloaf

Serves 6
Preparation Time: 10 minutes
Cooking Time: 25 minutes

- 1½ cups leftover cornbread, crumbled

- 1 lb. lean ground beef

- 10-oz. can enchilada sauce (I prefer mild but pick the hotness that you like)

- ½ cup shredded cheddar cheese

Combine the cornbread, beef, and all but ½ cup of the enchilada sauce in a mixing bowl. Mix until combined. Press into a loaf pan. Bake at 350° for 15 minutes. Remove the loaf from the oven and pour the ½ cup of enchilada sauce (that was set aside) over the meat. Sprinkle the cheese on top. Cook for an additional 10 minutes.

Cost per serving (1/6 of loaf): 65¢

NUTRITIONAL ANALYSIS PER SERVING
Calories: 343
Fat: 15 grams
Cholesterol: 82 mg
Carbohydrates: 28 grams
Fiber: 1 gram
Protein: 22 grams
Sodium: 891 mg

Kitchen Tip

Avoid OPENING THE OVEN DOOR while food is baking. Each time the door is opened, the oven temperature drops 25 to 35 degrees.

Lemon Artichoke Chicken

Serves 4
Preparation Time: 10 minutes
Cooking Time: 25 minutes

- ¾ cup Alfredo sauce
- ½ tsp. pepper
- 2 garlic cloves, crushed
- ½ cup lemon juice
- 6 oz. artichoke hearts
- ½ tsp. dried parsley
- ¾ cup seasoned bread crumbs (see page 210)
- ¼ cup Parmesan cheese
- 1 lb. chicken breasts (4 breasts)

In a small saucepan combine the Alfredo sauce, pepper, garlic, lemon juice, artichoke hearts, and parsley. Turn the heat to low and let the ingredients simmer, stirring occasionally. In a gallon-sized plastic bag, combine the bread crumbs and Parmesan. Put the chicken breasts in the bag with the bread crumbs and toss until the breasts are covered well. Put the breasts in a baking pan and bake in a preheated oven at 350° for 20 minutes or until cooked thoroughly in the center. Place the chicken on a plate and spoon the sauce over the chicken breast. If desired, serve over fettuccine noodles.

Cost per serving (4 oz. chicken plus sauce): 99¢

NUTRITIONAL ANALYSIS PER SERVING	
Calories: 368	
Fat: 12 grams	
Cholesterol: 85 mg	
Carbohydrates: 25 grams	
Fiber: 1 gram	
Protein: 38 grams	
Sodium: 1,025 mg	

Kitchen Tip

Sugar is made from either sugar beets or sugarcane and processed into several types of sugar. GRANULATED sugar is used in most recipes. BAKERS' SPECIAL is a finer grade of granulated sugar that dissolves fast. RAW sugar is the product that's left after sugarcane has been processed and refined. TURBINADO is raw sugar that has been "washed." BROWN sugar is granulated sugar that has had some molasses added back in.

Tuna Florentine

Serves 6
Preparation Time: 15 minutes
Cooking Time: 15 minutes

- 8 oz. egg noodles
- 16 oz. frozen spinach, thawed and drained
- 6-oz. can tuna, drained
- 2 cups grated cheddar cheese
- 1 tsp. onion powder
- 1 tsp. garlic powder
- ½ tsp. pepper
- ½ tsp. celery salt
- 1 T. lemon juice

NUTRITIONAL ANALYSIS PER SERVING	
Calories: 286	
Fat: 11 grams	
Cholesterol: 69 mg	
Carbohydrates: 24 grams	
Fiber: 3 grams	
Protein: 23 grams	
Sodium: 461 mg	

Boil the noodles according to package directions in a large saucepan. Drain. Add the rest of the ingredients to the noodles and mix well. Pour contents into an ungreased 9x13 pan. Bake at 325° for 10 to 15 minutes or until the center is warm.

Cost per serving (1 cup): 80¢

Kitchen Tip

The term FLORENTINE traces back to Florence, Italy, where a Florentine dish was an egg, fish, or meat dish served on a bed of spinach leaves and covered with a sauce.

Jam Chicken

Serves 4
Preparation Time: 10 minutes
Cooking Time: 30 minutes

- 2 T. jam*
- 3 T. low-sodium soy sauce
- 2 T. water
- 1 T. grated fresh ginger
- 1 lb. boneless, skinless chicken breast

NUTRITIONAL ANALYSIS PER SERVING
Calories: 134
Fat: 1 gram
Cholesterol: 53 mg
Carbohydrates: 8 grams
Fiber: 0 grams
Protein: 22 grams
Sodium: 426 mg

Combine the jam, soy sauce, water, and ginger in a large mixing bowl and mix well. Add the chicken and toss so that it is covered with sauce. Place the chicken on a baking sheet and bake for 30 minutes at 350°.

Note: For added flavor, let the chicken marinate in the sauce (covered in the refrigerator) for 2 to 3 hours before cooking.

Slow-Cooker Option: Place all ingredients in the pot, and cook on low for 4 hours.

*Almost any jam can be used and will taste good. My favorite is apricot jam. Marmalade and seedless berry jams also work well. Jelly does not work as well due to its thinner consistency.

Cost per serving (¼ lb.): 82¢

 *Kitchen Tip*

FRESH GINGERROOT has a much better flavor than powdered ginger. But if fresh ginger is unavailable, substitute as follows: Instead of 1 T. fresh ginger, use 1 tsp. powdered ginger + ¼ tsp. pepper + ½ tsp. lemon juice. Fresh gingerroot can be purchased in most produce departments. The skin must be peeled before grating or dicing the root. Wrapped in plastic wrap, the gingerroot can be stored in the refrigerator for 3 weeks or the freezer for 6 months. For ease of use, grate an entire gingerroot and store in an airtight container in the freezer. Remove what you need and leave the rest in the freezer. Fresh ginger should never be replaced with pickled or candied ginger in a recipe calling for gingerroot.

Blackened Fish

Serves 6
Preparation Time: 15 minutes
Cooking Time: 5 minutes

Open the windows and turn on the vent . . . this makes a lot of smoke!

- 1 T. paprika
- 1 tsp. onion powder
- ¾ tsp. cayenne powder
- 1 tsp. salt
- ½ tsp. black pepper
- 1 tsp. garlic powder
- ½ tsp. ground thyme
- ½ tsp. ground oregano
- ¼ tsp. cumin
- water or milk
- 3 T. butter
- 2 lbs. fish fillets (catfish, halibut, red snapper—don't use very thin fillets like sole)

NUTRITIONAL ANALYSIS PER SERVING
Calories: 182
Fat: 7 grams
Cholesterol: 80 mg
Carbohydrates: 2 grams
Fiber: 0 grams
Protein: 27 grams
Sodium: 496 mg

Combine all of the spices onto a plate or pie pan. In another pie pan or shallow dish, pour some water or milk for dipping the fish.

Melt the butter over high heat in a heavy metal or cast-iron skillet. Dip the fish into the milk or water, then dip it on both sides in the spices. Cook the fillets in the skillet for 2 to 3 minutes on each side. They will look burnt, but they'll taste great. The high heat is turning the spices into a crust and sealing the moisture in the fish.

Cost per serving (5 oz.): 93¢

Kitchen Tip

To put out a GREASE FIRE in a skillet, shake baking soda or salt on it until the fire is smothered (be careful not to get burned). Do not use flour, as it is flammable, or water, as it spreads the fire.

Boston Chicken

Serves 4
Preparation Time: 10 minutes
Cooking Time: 40 minutes

- ¼ tsp. paprika
- 1 T. lime juice
- 1 T. honey
- ¼ cup oil
- 1 lb. boneless, skinless chicken breasts

In a small bowl, combine the paprika, lime juice, honey, and oil. Mix well.

Place the chicken on a baking sheet lined with aluminum foil, and baste with some of the oil mixture. Bake at 400° for 30 to 40 minutes, basting every 10 minutes with the remaining mixture or until cooked through and the meat is not pink. Remove from oven and serve.

Cost per serving (¼ lb.): 91¢

NUTRITIONAL ANALYSIS PER SERVING

Calories: 267

Fat: 15 grams

Cholesterol: 66 mg

Carbohydrates: 5 grams

Fiber: 0 grams

Protein: 26 grams

Sodium: 78 mg

Kitchen Tip

PAPRIKA is made by grinding dried red peppers of varying heat, from sweet to hot. It is used to add flavor to all sorts of dishes, with some dishes (such as Hungarian goulash) calling for large amounts. It should be stored in a cool, dry place, as with other spices, for up to six months; after that it loses much of its flavor.

Tuna Loaf

Serves 4
Preparation Time: 10 minutes
Cooking Time: 30 minutes

- 2 6-oz. cans tuna in water, drained
- 2 egg whites
- ¼ cup milk
- 1 cup homemade bread crumbs (see page 210)
- ½ tsp. celery salt
- ¼ tsp. paprika
- 1 T. lemon juice
- 1 T. olive oil
- 3 T. dried parsley
- 2 T. chopped onion

NUTRITIONAL ANALYSIS PER SERVING	
Calories: 265	
Fat: 6 grams	
Cholesterol: 25 mg	
Carbohydrates: 22 grams	
Fiber: 2 grams	
Protein: 27 grams	
Sodium: 700 mg	

Combine all of the ingredients in a mixing bowl and mix well to distribute. Grease a bread loaf pan. Place the mixture in the pan. The loaf pan will be about half full. Bake at 400° for 30 minutes. Check after 20 minutes. If it is browning too fast on the top, reduce the heat to 350° for the remaining cooking time.

Cost per serving (¾ cup): 32¢

Kitchen Tip

When a recipe calls for FISH, any type can usually be used. If it calls for canned fish, any canned fish can be substituted (tuna, salmon, etc.). If using canned salmon, grind up the bones with the meat for added vitamins and minerals. There are five types of salmon. The best for salads or eating plain are Chinook/king, sockeye/red, and pink. The others (chum and coho/silver) are inferior tasting and are only good for recipes with many ingredients (stir-fry, salads, casseroles).

Chef Mis-er-ly Beefy Mac

Serves 8
Preparation Time: 10 minutes
Cooking Time: 15 minutes

- 1 lb. lean ground beef
- 10 oz. macaroni noodles
- 3 8-oz. cans tomato sauce
- ½ tsp. onion powder
- 1 tsp. paprika
- 1 tsp. Italian seasoning (see page 209)
- ½ tsp. garlic powder
- ¼ tsp. pepper
- salt to taste

NUTRITIONAL ANALYSIS PER SERVING

Calories: 239

Fat: 4 grams

Cholesterol: 33 mg

Carbohydrates: 34 grams

Fiber: 2 grams

Protein: 18 grams

Sodium: 591 mg

Brown the ground beef and drain off any fat. In a large saucepan, boil the noodles according to the package directions. Drain the noodles, add the beef to the noodles, and add the rest of the ingredients. Toss thoroughly and serve immediately.

This is great served with garlic bread.

Cost per serving (1 cup): 57¢

Kitchen Tip

Having the RIGHT-SIZE FRYING PAN makes cooking easier. Here's a helpful guide: an 8-inch pan is good for a small omelet or a grilled cheese sandwich; a 10-inch pan can handle four beef patties; a 12-inch pan can handle a stir-fry or one-dish meal.

Calzones

Serves 6
Preparation Time: 30 minutes
Cooking Time: 25 minutes

Dough:

- 2½ cups flour
- 1 cup water
- 1 T. oil
- 2¼ tsp. (or 1 pkg.) dry yeast
- 1 tsp. sugar
- 1 tsp. salt

Filling:

- 8 oz. chicken breast, cooked and diced
- 2 T. water chestnuts, drained and diced
- 1 T. chopped onion
- 2 T. mayonnaise
- 2 T. sour cream
- ¼ tsp. celery salt

NUTRITIONAL ANALYSIS PER SERVING
Calories: 295
Fat: 8 grams
Cholesterol: 22 mg
Carbohydrates: 42 grams
Fiber: 2 grams
Protein: 13 grams
Sodium: 479 mg

To save yourself the hassle of MAKING PIECRUSTS each time you need them, make several at one time. Double-wrap the dough in plastic wrap and freeze them. Do the same with pizza (or calzone) dough. They last 4 months in the freezer. To use, thaw and roll into desired shape.

Combine the dough ingredients in a bread machine (use the "dough" setting), or combine by hand and knead until elastic. Divide the dough into 6 balls. Roll each into a 6- or 7-inch circle on a floured surface.

In a separate bowl, combine the filling ingredients. Place 1/6 of the filling in the center of a dough circle, fold in half, and pinch the edges shut. Repeat with the other circles. Place the calzones on a baking sheet. Bake at 350° for 20 to 25 minutes or until golden brown.

Variations: Combine any meat, cheese, tofu, vegetables, scrambled egg, and spices to make the filling.

Calzones

(continued)

Keep the liquid to a minimum (e.g., use marinara sauce instead of fresh tomatoes) to avoid soggy dough.

Note: To make a quicker but more expensive version of this recipe, purchase ready-made unbaked piecrusts. Divide each circle in half, fill, pinch, and bake.

Cost per serving (1 calzone): 43¢

Orange Curry

Serves 4
Preparation Time: 15 minutes
Cooking Time: 15 minutes

This is a good recipe to use leftover meat.

- ½ cup frozen concentrated orange juice
- ⅓ cup + 1 T. water
- 1 T. curry powder
- 1 tsp. salt
- ½ cup minced onion
- 2 cloves garlic, pressed
- 1 T. oil
- 1 T. cornstarch
- 1 cup cooked, diced meat or substitute (chicken, beef, tofu, seitan, etc.)
- 1 cup steamed vegetables (broccoli, cauliflower, celery, mushrooms, potatoes, peas, etc.)

NUTRITIONAL ANALYSIS PER SERVING
Calories: 157
Fat: 4 grams
Cholesterol: 27 mg
Carbohydrates: 18 grams
Fiber: 1 gram
Protein: 12 grams
Sodium: 642 mg

In a saucepan over medium heat, combine the orange juice concentrate, ⅓ cup water, curry powder, salt, onion, garlic, and oil. In a separate small bowl, combine the cornstarch and 1 tablespoon of water. Mix well. Slowly whisk the cornstarch mixture into the orange juice mixture. Continue whisking the mixture as it simmers until it thickens (2 to 3 minutes).

Remove the sauce from the heat. Reheat the meat and vegetables (if cold) in the microwave. Toss with the sauce. If desired, serve over rice and garnish with orange slices.

Note: Make the sauce alone for a nice salad dressing.

Cost per serving (¾ cup): 68¢

Kitchen Tip

CURRY POWDER is a mixture of dried and crushed chili peppers blended with up to 20 various herbs and spices. Each chef or manufacturer has a unique blend. There are two main types of prepared curry powder: madras (hot style) and standard. The powder loses its flavor over time, so discard after 2 to 3 months.

Taco Salad

Serves 4
Preparation Time: 20 minutes
Cooking Time: 10 minutes

- ½ lb. lean ground beef
- ¼ medium onion, diced
- 2 cloves garlic, pressed
- 2 T. Mexican seasoning mix (see page 215)
- ¼ tsp. hot sauce (see page 204)
- ½ head lettuce (any type), shredded
- 5 oz. corn chips (½ of 10-oz. bag)
- ½ cup grated cheddar cheese
- 1 tomato, diced

NUTRITIONAL ANALYSIS PER SERVING
Calories: 351
Fat: 20 grams
Cholesterol: 48 mg
Carbohydrates: 25 grams
Fiber: 3 grams
Protein: 20 grams
Sodium: 649 mg

In a skillet, brown the ground beef over medium heat. Add the onion and garlic for the last 1 to 2 minutes of browning. Drain the beef. Add the Mexican seasoning and hot sauce to the beef. Mix well.

Place the lettuce on 4 serving plates. Top with the corn chips, the meat, the cheese, and the tomato.

Serve with salsa, guacamole, or sour cream if desired.

Cost per serving (1½ cups): 82¢

Kitchen Tip

CUTTING LETTUCE with a knife may cause the leaves to bruise and discolor. To avoid this, tear the leaves instead.

Enchilito

(Enchilada-Burrito)

Serves 8
Preparation Time: 20 minutes
Cooking Time: 10 minutes

- 1 lb. lean ground beef
- ¼ cup flour
- 1 tsp. chili powder
- ⅓ cup diced onion
- 4 cloves garlic, pressed
- ½ tsp. salt
- ½ cup water
- 16-oz. can fat-free refried beans
- 10 fat-free flour tortillas (7-inch)
- 1½ cups hot sauce (see page 204)
- 1½ cups grated cheddar cheese

NUTRITIONAL ANALYSIS PER SERVING	
Calories: 440	
Fat: 23 grams	
Cholesterol: 79 mg	
Carbohydrates: 44 grams	
Fiber: 5 grams	
Protein: 25 grams	
Sodium: 818 mg	

Brown the beef in a skillet. Remove from heat and drain. Return the meat to the skillet and add the flour, chili powder, onion, garlic, and salt. Toss to mix the spices evenly. Add the water and stir over medium heat for 8 to 10 minutes or until smooth and creamy.

In a separate pan warm the refried beans over low to medium heat for 2 to 3 minutes. Remove from the heat.

Place about 3 tablespoons of refried beans and 3 tablespoons of ground beef on each tortilla. Fold the tortilla sides in and over the beef, then flip the tortilla over so the folded side is down. Place it on a microwave-safe plate. Cover each enchilito with 2 to 3 tablespoons of hot sauce and 2 heaping tablespoons of cheese. Heat the dish in the microwave on high for 30 to 40 seconds, or until the cheese melts. Repeat with the rest of the tortillas.

Cost per serving (1 to 2 enchilitos): 92¢

Kitchen Tip

To CHOP LOTS OF ONIONS at one time, cut one onion into six pieces, place in a blender, cover with water, and blend for 15 seconds or until the pieces are tiny. Pour out into a large strainer. Repeat with additional onions. Store any unused portion in an airtight container for a future use. This can also be frozen.

Spanish Potato

Serves 4
Preparation Time: 1 hour, 15 minutes
Cooking Time: 5 minutes

- 4 large potatoes
- ½ lb. lean ground beef
- ¼ tsp. chili powder
- ¼ cup diced onion
- 3 cloves garlic, pressed
- ½ tsp. Tabasco sauce
- 6 oz. tomato sauce
- ¾ cup grated cheddar cheese

Bake the potatoes at 425° (or microwave) until tender in the center. Cut each potato in half lengthwise, and then scoop out the center of each potato with a spoon, being careful not to cut into the skin. Place the potato pulp in a large mixing bowl.

Brown the ground beef in a skillet. Drain the beef. Add the beef to the bowl with the potato pulp. Add the chili powder, onion, garlic, Tabasco sauce, and tomato sauce. Mix well.

Stuff the potato shells with the potato-meat mixture. It will be heaping out of the skins. Sprinkle 3 tablespoons of cheese over the top of each potato. Place the potatoes on a cookie sheet, and return to the oven for 2 to 3 minutes to melt the cheese.

Cost per serving (1 filled potato): 69¢

NUTRITIONAL ANALYSIS PER SERVING	
Calories: 351	
Fat: 18 grams	
Cholesterol: 63 mg	
Carbohydrates: 33 grams	
Fiber: 4 grams	
Protein: 20 grams	
Sodium: 510 mg	

Kitchen Tip

TABASCO SAUCE is made from a hot Tabasco pepper. The pepper is only grown in Central America and Louisiana. The peppers are made into a mash, and then fermented for three years before being made into the zesty sauce by blending the peppers with vinegar and salt. One family has owned the recipe and brand name since the 1800s.

Salmon Cakes

Serves 4
Preparation Time: 10 minutes
Cooking Time: 10 minutes

- 14-oz. can salmon
- 2 T. flour or homemade bread crumbs (see page 210)
- 2 T. lemon juice
- 1 egg
- 1 tsp. Italian seasoning (see page 209)
- ¼ tsp. pepper
- ½ tsp. garlic powder
- ½ tsp. onion powder
- 2 tsp. oil

<table>
<tr><th colspan="2">NUTRITIONAL ANALYSIS
PER SERVING</th></tr>
<tr><td>Calories:</td><td>195</td></tr>
<tr><td>Fat:</td><td>10 grams</td></tr>
<tr><td>Cholesterol:</td><td>100 mg</td></tr>
<tr><td>Carbohydrates:</td><td>5 grams</td></tr>
<tr><td>Fiber:</td><td>0 grams</td></tr>
<tr><td>Protein:</td><td>22 grams</td></tr>
<tr><td>Sodium:</td><td>564 mg</td></tr>
</table>

Drain the salmon and place the meat in a medium mixing bowl. Remove the bones and skin.

Add all the remaining ingredients except the oil to the salmon and mix well so everything is evenly distributed. Form into four patties.

Heat the oil in a large skillet on medium heat. Cook the patties in the skillet for 3 to 5 minutes on each side.

Serve on a bun with lettuce and other condiments.

Cost per serving (1 patty): 53¢

Kitchen Tip

A quick SUBSTITUTE FOR LEMON JUICE is vinegar. Use an equal amount in its place. The type of vinegar does not matter, unless a great deal of lemon juice is called for (if this is the case, do not substitute).

White Lasagna

Serves 4
Preparation Time: 30 minutes
Cooking Time: 20 minutes

- 1 cup diced cooked beef or chicken
- 1 cup diced broccoli
- 1 cup frozen chopped spinach, thawed and drained
- 8 lasagna noodles, cooked and drained

Sauce:

- ¼ cup oil
- ¼ cup flour
- 2 cups milk
- 1 T. basil
- 2 tsp. garlic powder
- 1 tsp. onion powder
- ½ tsp. each salt and pepper
- 1 T. Italian seasoning (see page 209)
- ½ cup grated Monterey Jack cheese

NUTRITIONAL ANALYSIS PER SERVING	
Calories: 270	
Fat: 14 grams	
Cholesterol: 30 mg	
Carbohydrates: 22 grams	
Fiber: 2 grams	
Protein: 16 grams	
Sodium: 312 mg	

To make the sauce, heat the oil in a medium sauce-pan, and add the flour to form a paste. Add the milk and all the remaining sauce ingredients. Bring to a simmer, stirring constantly. Continue to simmer and stir until it thickens. Remove from heat and set aside. In a separate bowl, combine the meat, broccoli, and spinach.

Place 2 of the noodles on the bottom of an 8x8 baking pan. Add ¼ of the meat mixture and evenly distribute over the noodles, then cover with ¼ of the sauce. Repeat this layering until all the ingredients are used. Bake uncovered at 350° for 20 minutes.

Cost per serving (1½ cups): 72¢

Kitchen Tip

To REDUCE FAT in a recipe that calls for sautéing onion and garlic in oil, replace the oil with twice as much broth or water. Place the liquid in a skillet or saucepan, heat to simmering, add vegetables, and cover. Let simmer for 1 to 2 minutes or until the onion or garlic is soft. Add a little more liquid if all the liquid evaporates. Proceed with the recipe as specified.

Chinese Chicken Salad

Serves 4
Preparation Time: 20 minutes

- ¼ cup oil
- 1 pkg. chicken-flavored ramen noodles
- 2 T. vinegar (rice or wine)
- 1 T. low-sodium soy sauce
- 1 head iceberg lettuce
- ½ bunch green onions
- 1 boneless, skinless chicken breast, cooked and cubed

NUTRITIONAL ANALYSIS PER SERVING

Calories: 239

Fat: 18 grams

Cholesterol: 13 mg

Carbohydrates: 18 grams

Fiber: 3 grams

Protein: 9 grams

Sodium: 547 mg

In a small saucepan, combine the oil, flavor packet from the ramen noodles, vinegar, and soy sauce. Mix well and heat until warm. Remove from the heat.

Shred the lettuce into thin strips. Place in a large salad bowl. Thinly slice the green onions, and add them to the salad bowl. Break up the uncooked ramen noodles into the salad bowl. Add the chicken. Toss well. Drizzle the dressing over the salad and toss again. Serve immediately.

Note: Most ramen noodles have MSG (monosodium glutamate) in the flavor packet, but they can be purchased without MSG at health food stores.

Options: For added flavor, toss in ¼ cup sliced almonds or a 6-oz. can of mandarin oranges.

Cost per serving (1½ cups): 79¢

 *Kitchen Tip*

RAMEN NOODLES are Asian noodles that have been deep fried in oil, and then dried. They are usually sold in packages with seasoning to add to the cooking water for soup. Low-fat versions are also available.

Basic Freezer Meatballs

Serves 6
Preparation Time: 20 minutes
Cooking Time: 15 minutes

- 1 lb. lean ground beef
- ½ cup oats
- ¼ onion, diced
- ½ tsp. garlic powder
- ½ tsp. salt
- ¼ tsp. pepper
- 1½ tsp. flour
- ½ tsp. Worcestershire sauce
- ¼ cup water
- 2 T. Italian seasoning (see page 209)

NUTRITIONAL ANALYSIS PER SERVING	
Calories: 233	
Fat: 14 grams	
Cholesterol: 52 mg	
Carbohydrates: 10 grams	
Fiber: 0 grams	
Protein: 17 grams	
Sodium: 78 mg	

Combine all of the ingredients in a large mixing bowl. Mix well with your hands or a mixer. Shape into 36 1-inch meatballs. Place on a baking sheet. Bake at 350° for 15 minutes.

Remove from oven and place on a plate lined with paper towels to drain the fat. Move the meatballs to a cookie sheet or other tray that can be placed in the freezer. Don't let them touch each other on the tray. Freeze overnight. Place the meatballs in a freezer bag, squeeze the excess air out of the bag (to avoid freezer burn), and return to freezer. Store for up to 4 months.

Use in any recipe that calls for meatballs. (Try with sweet and sour sauce [page 198] or spaghetti sauce [page 205]).

Cost per serving (6 meatballs): 29¢

Kitchen Tip

The TYPE OF ONION used may affect the flavor of your dish. The BERMUDA and SPANISH onion are the most common yellow-skinned onions found in nearly all grocery stores. The WHITE onion has a mild flavor and can be used where yellow ones are called for. The VIDALIA onion is very sweet and juicy. The RED (or Italian) onion is sweet and mild.

Chicken 'n' Dumplings

Serves 6
Preparation Time: 10 minutes
Cooking Time: 20 minutes

- 1 lb. boneless, skinless chicken breasts
- 1 cup chicken broth
- 2 carrots, diced
- 2 celery stalks, diced
- 2 T. oil
- ¼ cup flour
- ½ cup milk
- ½ tsp. pepper
- ½ tsp. Italian seasoning (see page 209)
- 1 can biscuit dough (10 biscuits)

NUTRITIONAL ANALYSIS PER SERVING	
Calories: 378	
Fat: 11 grams	
Cholesterol: 45 mg	
Carbohydrates: 44 grams	
Fiber: 1 gram	
Protein: 26 grams	
Sodium: 848 mg	

Cut the chicken into large pieces. Place in a large saucepan with the chicken broth and vegetables, and simmer until chicken and vegetables are tender (about 5 to 10 minutes).

While this is cooking, combine the oil and flour in a small saucepan to form a paste. Add the milk and spices, and then heat over medium heat until it begins to thicken, while stirring constantly.

Pour the sauce into the pan with the chicken and vegetables. Stir until the sauce is blended into the chicken mixture. Place the biscuit dough over the chicken pieces, cover the pan, and simmer for 10 minutes or until the biscuits are done.

Cost per serving (1 cup): 52¢

 Kitchen Tip

DUMPLINGS are any dough boiled or steamed on top of another dish. Cook pastry dough on top of a moist fruit recipe for a dessert dumpling. Or poach sweet dough over a sweet cream sauce. Dumplings can be filled with meat as well.

Salmon Pasta Delight

Serves 6
Preparation Time: 25 minutes
Cooking Time: 10 minutes

- 4 cups cooked pasta (bow ties, egg noodles, etc.)
- 15-oz. can salmon
- 1½ cups frozen mixed vegetables, cooked
- 1 tsp. celery salt
- ½ tsp. curry powder
- 1 tsp. onion powder
- 1 tsp. garlic powder
- ½ tsp. pepper
- 1 cup grated cheddar cheese
- 2 T. oil
- ¼ cup flour
- 2 cups milk

NUTRITIONAL ANALYSIS PER SERVING	
Calories: 341	
Fat: 15 grams	
Cholesterol: 60 mg	
Carbohydrates: 35 grams	
Fiber: 4 grams	
Protein: 18 grams	
Sodium: 587 mg	

Drain the salmon, remove and discard any skin or bones, and crumble the fish over the pasta. Add the vegetables, and sprinkle the spices and cheese over the noodle mix.

In a small saucepan, mix the flour and oil to form a paste. Add the milk and cook over medium heat, stirring constantly, until thick. Pour over the noodle mixture and blend well. This can be served immediately if the dish has remained warm. If it has cooled, pour the mix into a 9x13 pan and heat at 350° for 10 minutes.

Cost per serving (1 cup): 71¢

Kitchen Tip

ROUX (pronounced "roo") is a combination of flour and fat (butter, oil, or drippings) used as a thickening agent for soups, stews, and sauces. A variety of ingredients can be added to roux once it has been started: spices, cheese, milk, broth, etc. If your recipe needs thickening, make a roux and mix it into the liquid.

Tuna Pastry

Serves 8
Preparation Time: 30 minutes
Cooking Time: 10 to 15 minutes

Filling:

- 2 6-oz. cans tuna, drained
- ¼ cup diced celery
- 2 T. light mayonnaise
- 2 T. diced onion
- ¼ cup grated cheddar cheese
- 1 T. lemon juice
- 1 tsp. dill
- ¼ tsp. pepper

Dough:

- 2 cups flour
- 1 T. baking powder
- 1 tsp. sugar
- ½ tsp. salt
- ¾ cup milk
- ½ cup cold butter or shortening

Mix all of the ingredients for the filling in a large mixing bowl. Set aside.

In another large mixing bowl, stir together all the dough ingredients except the butter. Mix the butter in with a pastry cutter or two knives, continually cutting the butter into smaller and smaller pieces. Once they are small like peas, work the dough with your hands. Roll it out to ¼-inch thickness on a floured board. Cut into 3-inch-diameter circles.

Place one heaping teaspoon of the filling in the

NUTRITIONAL ANALYSIS PER SERVING	
Calories: 286	
Fat: 13 grams	
Cholesterol: 48 mg	
Carbohydrates: 27 grams	
Fiber: 0 grams	
Protein: 15 grams	
Sodium: 199 mg	

Kitchen Tip

TUNA can usually be replaced with any canned fish or meat. Try salmon, canned chicken, or even deviled ham.

Tuna Pastry

(continued)

center of a dough round. Place another dough round on top and pinch the edges closed. Repeat with the remaining dough. Place on an ungreased cookie sheet. Bake at 350° for 10 to 15 minutes, or until the pastries are golden brown.

Cost per serving (2 to 3 each): 26¢

Broccoli Beef

Serves 4
Preparation Time: 15 minutes
Cooking Time: 10 minutes

- ¼ cup low-sodium soy sauce
- 1 T. peanut butter (chunky or smooth)
- ¼ tsp. hot sauce (see page 204)
- ½ cup water
- 1 T. cornstarch
- 2 tsp. vinegar
- ¼ tsp. pepper
- ⅛ tsp. powdered ginger
- ½ tsp. garlic powder
- ½ tsp. onion powder
- 2 T. oil
- ½ lb. diced or cubed beef (or any meat)
- 2 cups broccoli cut into small pieces

In a small bowl, combine the soy sauce, peanut butter, hot sauce, water, cornstarch, vinegar, pepper, ginger, garlic powder, and onion powder. Mix well and set aside.

In a large skillet or wok, heat the oil over medium-high heat. Add the beef and cook, stirring constantly, for 2 to 3 minutes. Add the broccoli and stir for another 2 to 3 minutes. Add the sauce and mix thoroughly, then continue to stir as the sauce thickens. Once it thickens, remove from the heat.

Serve immediately with steamed rice or fried rice (see page 68).

Cost per serving (1 cup): 73¢

NUTRITIONAL ANALYSIS PER SERVING
Calories: 184
Fat: 12 grams
Cholesterol: 33 mg
Carbohydrates: 5 grams
Fiber: 1 gram
Protein: 15 grams
Sodium: 540 mg

Kitchen Tip

STIR-FRY is a cooking term that comes from Asian cooking. It refers to a style of cooking that involves high heat and quick stirring action. This style requires little oil and allows the vegetables to remain crisp. It is best accomplished with the use of a wok—a bowl-shaped pan—which allows you to stir the ingredients quickly.

Popover Pizza

Serves 4
Preparation Time: 15 minutes
Cooking Time: 20 minutes

- ½ lb. lean ground beef
- ½ onion, diced
- 1 cup spaghetti sauce (see page 205)
- ½ cup grated Monterey Jack or mozzarella cheese

Crust:

- 2 egg whites
- ½ cup milk
- ½ cup flour
- ¼ tsp. salt

In a large skillet, brown the ground beef and onion. Remove from heat and drain the excess fat. Add the spaghetti sauce and cheese to the skillet. Toss to mix evenly. Pour into an 8x8 pan and distribute evenly in the pan.

Combine all of the crust ingredients in a mixing bowl. Mix well. Pour over the meat and spread around to cover evenly.

Bake at 400° for 20 minutes, or until the crust is a light golden brown.

Note: To reduce the fat and cholesterol, replace the hamburger with TVP (see note in "Vegetarian Main Dishes" chapter).

Cost per serving (4-inch square): 48¢

NUTRITIONAL ANALYSIS PER SERVING	
Calories: 321	
Fat: 16 grams	
Cholesterol: 53 mg	
Carbohydrates: 23 grams	
Fiber: 3 grams	
Protein: 20 grams	
Sodium: 623 mg	

Kitchen Tip

MONTEREY JACK CHEESE is a mild white cheese. It is also called California Jack, Sonoma Jack, and Jack cheese. It originated in Monterey, California. It is not usually aged, giving it a mild flavor and very soft texture.

Tandoori Chicken

Serves 4
Preparation Time: 10 minutes + marinating time
Cooking Time: 35 minutes
Recipe donated by Joan Stivers

- 1 lb. boneless, skinless chicken, cubed
- 1 cup plain yogurt
- 2 cloves garlic, pressed
- 1½ tsp. ginger powder
- 1 tsp. paprika
- 1 T. lemon juice
- 1 T. curry powder*
- ½ tsp. salt

NUTRITIONAL ANALYSIS PER SERVING

Calories: 176	
Fat: 4 grams	
Cholesterol: 73 mg	
Carbohydrates: 5 grams	
Fiber: 1 gram	
Protein: 29 grams	
Sodium: 371 mg	

Combine all of the ingredients except the chicken in a medium mixing bowl. Mix well. Add the chicken and toss so the chicken is evenly coated. Cover and marinate in the refrigerator for 4 to 6 hours. This can also be made the night before.

Place the chicken on a baking pan. Reserve ½ cup of marinade in the bowl. Cover the chicken with foil, and bake at 400° for 20 minutes. Baste the chicken with the remaining marinade, reduce the heat to 350°, and bake uncovered for an additional 15 minutes.

Serve with rice seasoned with cumin.

Note: This chicken tastes best when grilled over a barbecue—just cut larger cubes. Marinate as directed. Grill the meat until cooked thoroughly, basting during the last 10 minutes of cooking.

*If you don't have curry powder, use 1 T. ground cumin + ½ tsp. cinnamon + ½ tsp. cloves in its place.

Cost per serving (¼ lb.): 82¢

Kitchen Tip

CUMIN is the seed of a plant in the parsley family. It has a nutty and peppery flavor and complements most meats and vegetables. It is widely used in Asian, Middle Eastern, and Mexican cooking, and is also used to make curries and chili powder. It can be purchased in most grocery stores.

Baked Chicken Nuggets

Serves 4
Preparation Time: 10 minutes
Cooking Time: 15 minutes

- 1 lb. boneless, skinless chicken
- ¼ cup low-fat mayonnaise
- 1 cup homemade bread crumbs (see page 210)
- ½ tsp. garlic powder
- ½ tsp. paprika
- 2 tsp. Italian seasoning (see page 209)
- ½ tsp. salt

Cut the chicken into 1-inch-wide strips. Pat them dry with a paper towel. Brush them with the mayonnaise.

Combine the rest of the ingredients in a shallow dish. Roll the chicken strips in the seasoning, then place on a baking sheet. Bake at 425° for 15 minutes.

Variation: Substitute 1 cup of shake-on chicken coating (page 211) for the bread crumbs, garlic powder, and Italian seasoning.

Cost per serving (¼ lb.): 74¢

NUTRITIONAL ANALYSIS PER SERVING
Calories: 234
Fat: 7 grams
Cholesterol: 53 mg
Carbohydrates: 17 grams
Fiber: 1 gram
Protein: 24 grams
Sodium: 514 mg

Kitchen Tip

MAYONNAISE is traditionally made by blending oil, eggs, vinegar, salt, and powdered mustard. The prepared mayonnaise sold in stores also has preservatives added to prevent spoiling. Low-fat versions add sugar and other ingredients to imitate the flavor and texture of the oil. To MAKE YOUR OWN LOW-FAT MAYONNAISE, combine equal parts of regular mayonnaise with fat-free sour cream or plain yogurt.

Easy Cajun Catfish

Serves 4
Preparation Time: 10 minutes
Cooking Time: 10 minutes

- ¼ cup milk
- ½ tsp. vinegar (any type)
- 2 tsp. prepared mustard (Dijon is best)
- ½ cup cornmeal
- ½ tsp. salt
- 1 tsp. paprika
- 1 tsp. onion powder
- ½ tsp. garlic powder
- ½ tsp. cayenne pepper
- ½ tsp. pepper
- ½ tsp. Italian seasoning (see page 209)
- 1½ lbs. catfish fillets
- lemon juice

NUTRITIONAL ANALYSIS PER SERVING

Calories: 186

Fat: 4 grams

Cholesterol: 66 mg

Carbohydrates: 16 grams

Fiber: 2 grams

Protein: 21 grams

Sodium: 356 mg

Prepare a baking rack or baking sheet with cooking spray or by brushing on oil. Preheat the oven to "broil."

Mix the milk, vinegar, and mustard in a shallow dish or pie plate. Whisk to evenly blend. In another shallow dish or pie plate combine the cornmeal with the seasonings.

Dip each fillet into the milk mixture, getting both sides wet, then dip both sides into the cornmeal mixture. Place the fish on the prepared baking sheet or rack and place in the oven 4 inches from the broiler. Cook for 3 to 5 minutes per side or until done in the center.

Serve with lemon juice.

Cost per serving (6 oz.): 66¢

 Kitchen Tip

FISH are categorized by their habitat: FRESHWATER or SALT-WATER. They are further categorized by their basic structure: flat or round. A flat fish swims on the bottom of the sea, has a flat body, and has both eyes on one side of its body, like a Dover sole. A round fish has a round body and one eye on each side of the head, like a trout.

Helping Hamburger

Serves 4
Preparation Time: 5 minutes
Cooking Time: 25 minutes

- 1 lb. lean ground beef
- 1 cup uncooked macaroni
- 15-oz. can tomato sauce
- ⅓ cup onion soup mix (see page 221)
- 1½ cups water

In a large skillet over medium heat, brown the hamburger. Drain the fat. Add the remaining ingredients. Stir to mix well, cover, and reduce heat to simmer. Simmer for 15 minutes or until the noodles are tender.

Variations:

- *Cheesy macaroni*: Add ½ cup grated cheddar cheese during the last 5 minutes of cooking time.
- *Mexican macaroni*: Add 1 tsp. Mexican seasoning mix (see page 215), omit the noodles, and serve over tortilla or corn chips.
- *Stroganoff*: Replace the tomato sauce with 1 cup sour cream, and replace the macaroni with wide egg noodles.

Cost per serving (1½ cups): 61¢

NUTRITIONAL ANALYSIS PER SERVING	
Calories: 216	
Fat: 4 grams	
Cholesterol: 44 mg	
Carbohydrates: 25 grams	
Fiber: 2 grams	
Protein: 21 grams	
Sodium: 490 mg	

 *Kitchen Tip*

To reduce the fat content in a recipe that contains GROUND BEEF, place the cooked ground beef in a colander and run hot water over it. This will wash away 20 to 30 percent of the excess fat.

CHAPTER 7

Vegetarian Main Dishes

VEGETARIAN COOKING

Why would you want to include a vegetarian meal in your menu plan if you're not a dedicated vegetarian? Two reasons: health and frugality. Despite criticisms that vegetarian meals are high in carbohydrates, high in fat, and low in protein, this does not have to be the case. Meals that revolve around produce, legumes, grains, and soy products tend to be low in price, low in fat, and filled with nutrients. With their nutritional value and low cost, I recommend adding a few vegetarian meals to the family menu.

Frugal vegetarian meals are not just potatoes, pastas, and breads. Nor are they limited to beans and rice. With some creativity, you can create a low-fat, high-protein, low-carbohydrate meal. And often it doesn't take a large portion of a legume-based meal to provide the protein needed. As discussed in chapter 1, we need a small amount of protein at each meal. Eating only what is needed for adequate protein, carbohydrates, vegetables, fruits, and grains maintains the overall healthiness of the meal. If you need or want to watch your carbohydrates, using tofu and seitan (see page 114) instead of legumes in your meals will accomplish your dietary goal and keep the meal frugal.

Meats, fish, milk, cheese, tofu, tempeh (see page 115), seitan, and eggs contain complete proteins. Most vegetarian meals provide the complete protein that the body needs. A complete protein is a combination of all of the essential amino acids that your body needs. Amino acids, extracted during digestion, are the building blocks that build and repair cells and tissue. Most plant sources do not provide all of the essential amino acids (soy products are an exception). Different types of plant sources with different amino acids are needed to form a complete protein. These do not have to be eaten at the same meal. For instance, baked beans (a legume) at lunch combined with brown rice (a grain) at dinner would form a complete protein.

According to nutrition expert and registered dietician Dr. Reed Mangles, PhD, in his coauthored book *Simply Vegan: Quick Vegetarian Meals* (Vegetarian Resource Group, 1999), we need to combine *unrefined* (whole) grains to make a complete protein combination. When manufacturers refine a grain, they remove many of the vitamins, minerals, essential fatty acids, and other nutrients. In other words, if we combine *white* rice with beans, it is not a complete protein—it needs to be brown rice. The same goes for whole wheat breads: they need to be 100 percent whole *grain* breads. Often bread manufacturers remove much of the wheat and replace a portion of it to add fiber or color. Make sure that the ingredient list includes "100% whole wheat flour." If it says simply "whole wheat flour," it may only be part of the wheat.

If you want to try a few meatless dishes, here are some guidelines to make sure that you are getting the right combinations to form a complete protein.

Complete Protein Combinations

whole grains + legumes
legumes + nuts or seeds
vegetables + legumes

Legumes are plants that have pods with rows of seeds inside. Some examples are chickpeas, beans (kidney, lima, garbanzo, etc.), lentils, peanuts, and alfalfa.

Examples of some *whole grains* are amaranth, quinoa (pronounced KEEN-wa), millet, buckwheat, brown rice, rye, oats, wheat, barley, spelt, and corn.

Please note that nuts and grains do not form a complete protein. Also note that peanuts are not in the nut category, but are legumes.

Some examples of the above combinations are:

WHOLE GRAINS + LEGUMES

- lentil and brown rice casserole
- brown rice and beans
- whole-grain pita bread and hummus
- beans with whole-grain pasta
- baked beans and brown (whole-grain) bread
- black-eyed peas and brown rice
- peanut butter and jelly sandwich on whole-grain bread
- corn and lima beans (succotash)
- refried beans on a whole-grain tortilla
- falafel
- corn bread and pinto beans

- bean burrito on a corn tortilla
- corn tortilla and beans
- black-bean soup and a whole-grain roll

LEGUMES + NUTS OR SEEDS

- cashew and peanut butter sandwich
- bean and walnut salad
- lentil and sunflower seed loaf
- beans and sesame seeds

VEGETABLES + LEGUMES

- bean and vegetable soup
- cashew and vegetable stir-fry
- eggplant and lentil casserole
- broccoli and garbanzo beans

To keep your vegetarian meal healthy, avoid fried foods, use egg whites instead of whole eggs, and go light on the cheese, using it just for a bit of flavor. Use fresh and raw produce as often as possible since cooking significantly reduces vital nutrients.

Common Vegetarian Foods

Lentils have been used for centuries as a meat substitute. They are an incomplete protein high in calcium, vitamins A and B, iron, and phosphorous. Lentils come in several colors, but they all taste and cook the same. The gray-brown lentil is from Europe, the red lentil is from Egypt, and the yellow lentil is from the Middle East. The dried seed can be stored for up to a year. Lentils do not have to be presoaked. Cook by boiling 1 cup of lentils in 2½ cups water for 40 minutes.

Dried beans are legumes and come in many varieties, including red, kidney, soy, garbanzo, white (or navy), pinto, lima, and black. They are an incomplete protein that is a fair source of vitamin B, carbohydrates, and minerals. They all require presoaking in order to begin the breakdown of their carbohydrates. There are two ways to presoak: overnight (12 hours), or quick (1 hour). In both methods, cover the beans with three times their volume in water (3:1 ratio of water to beans). Discard any beans that float. For the quick method, bring the water and beans to a boil, remove from the heat, cover, and let sit for an hour. For the overnight method, let the beans soak for about 12 hours, then drain and cook as the recipe directs. With either method, discarding the soaking water before cooking reduces gas problems that some people experience after eating beans. Beans can be cooked and then frozen for later use. One cup of dry beans equals 3 cups of cooked beans.

Tofu is a curd made from soymilk (or ground soybeans), prepared much like cheese. The whey from the soymilk is pressed out and the curd is formed into cakes or blocks. The more whey that is pressed out, the firmer the tofu. Tofu is a complete protein and is low in calories, low in fat, low in sodium, high in protein, and free of cholesterol. There are different types of tofu to choose from: silken, extra firm, firm, and soft. *Silken tofu* has a very smooth texture, much like custard. *Extra firm tofu* is dense and can be sliced, cubed, and even barbecued. *Firm tofu* has a bit more water and is a bit softer than extra firm but not as soft as silken. *Soft tofu* has the most water and is very soft, but still firmer than silken (silken tofu is best for puddings and sauces). Tofu is a versatile food that can be sliced, diced, mashed, fried, grilled, baked, or creamed. Tofu has no flavor of its own so it will taste like the seasonings you put on it. Tofu lasts for about two weeks when covered with water and refrigerated. It can be frozen for up to three months, but the texture will change after thawing. Once thawed, squeeze the excess moisture out with your hands, and crumble it to look like ground beef.

Seitan is often called "wheat meat" because it has the appearance and texture of meat and is made from wheat gluten. Wheat gluten, also known as vital gluten, is extracted from wheat, dried, and packaged for sale. It is not to be confused with gluten flour. The vital gluten is formed into dough, boiled with spices, and then prepared as you would meat (fried, baked, grilled, stewed, etc.)—see the recipe on page 122. You can also purchase seitan already prepared, but it is much more expensive to buy it than to make it. It is a complete protein that is low in calories, low in carbohydrates, high in protein, fat free, cholesterol free, and sodium free. Even though it is made from a grain (wheat), it is a complete protein because it is cooked in soy sauce, which provides the missing amino acid (lysine).

Tempeh is a cake made from fermented soybeans. It has a mild yeast flavor. It is a complete protein that is low in cholesterol, sodium, and fat, but high in protein. It is difficult to make and expensive to buy, therefore I do not use it in my cooking. However, some people prefer the taste of tempeh to tofu or seitan. If this is the case, it can be used wherever a recipe calls for seitan, tofu, or any meat.

TVP, or *texturized vegetable protein,* is made from soybeans. TVP is a complete protein that is low in fat, high in protein, high in fiber, and high in potassium, magnesium, and calcium. It's also inexpensive (it costs around 40¢ a pound, when hydrated). It is very versatile and can be used anywhere meat is used, but like tofu, it has no flavor; it assumes the flavor of the seasonings you use. It comes in many sizes: granules like ground beef, small chunks like beef cubes, and large chunks like chicken breast portions. It is sold dried and needs to be reconstituted with equal parts of hot water and TVP.

HOW TO INTRODUCE VEGETARIAN MEALS TO A RELUCTANT FAMILY

Many people balk at the thought of a vegetarian meal. Most of the problems are in their head, not their palate. So our challenge is to convince them that these alternative protein sources taste good.

Most families are comfortable with the meals they have most often, and they don't want to give them up for strange new recipes. Instead of overhauling the entire menu, and possibly causing a mutiny, simply modify what's already being served. Most of the time the family will accept it. Perhaps spelling out the nutritional (reduced calories, fat, and cholesterol) and monetary benefits will be an incentive to agree to a change.

Here are a few ideas to modify your existing meals:

- Make lasagna or other casseroles meatless by replacing the meat with TVP, thawed and crumbled tofu, or cooked bulgur (a quick-cooking form of whole wheat) or by adding sliced vegetables (zucchini, spinach, etc.) to the layers.

- On soup-and-bread night, make a meatless soup.

- On salad night, omit the diced meat and sprinkle the salad with a variety of beans (garbanzo, kidney, white, red, black, etc.) and some diced or shredded cheese.

- On pizza night, skip the meats and add more sliced and diced vegetables (bell pepper, black olive, zucchini, red onion, etc.).

- Use crumbled tofu instead of ricotta cheese or cottage cheese in a recipe.

- Omit the meat in chili, and either use more beans or replace the meat with seitan pieces (see recipe on page 122), TVP, or thawed and crumbled tofu.

- Replace the meat in tacos, stuffed bell peppers, and stuffed cabbage rolls with TVP, cooked bulgur, or thawed and crumbled tofu.

- If your family insists on having meat at each meal, try stretching the meat using 50 percent meat and 50 percent alternative.

I have included several of my favorite meat-free dishes in this chapter for you to sample. I hope you will try them and see how they help your health and your wallet.

Meatless Meatloaf

Serves 8
Preparation Time: 20 minutes
Cooking Time: 45 minutes

- 3 cups TVP granules
- 2½ cups boiling water
- ¼ cup ketchup
- 2 T. broth powder (see page 226)
- ¾ cup whole wheat flour
- ½ cup diced onion
- 1 tsp. salt
- ¼ tsp. pepper
- 3 cloves garlic, pressed
- 2 tsp. Italian seasoning mix (see page 209)

NUTRITIONAL ANALYSIS PER SERVING	
Calories: 155	
Fat: 0 grams	
Cholesterol: 0 mg	
Carbohydrates: 22 grams	
Fiber: 8 grams	
Protein: 20 grams	
Sodium: 396 mg	

Mix the TVP, boiling water, and ketchup in a bowl, and let sit for 10 minutes to soften the TVP. Add the remaining ingredients to the TVP and mix well.

Grease a loaf pan and pack the TVP mixture into the pan. Bake at 350° for 30 to 45 minutes. Begin checking it at 30 minutes. If it gets too brown on the top, cover it with foil for the remaining 15 minutes.

Remove from the oven, slice, and serve. If desired, serve with a mushroom gravy or marinara sauce. This is also excellent sliced and served as a sandwich on bread with ketchup and mayonnaise.

Cost per serving (¾ cup, 1 slice): 12¢

Kitchen Tip

To MIX A MEATLOAF without using your hands, use a potato masher to combine the ingredients.

Veggie Spaghetti Sauce

Serves 8
Preparation Time: 20 minutes
Cooking Time: 30 minutes
Recipe donated by Brynda Filkins

- 2 medium carrots, grated
- 1 zucchini, grated
- ½ bell pepper, diced
- 1 onion, minced
- 2 tomatoes, diced
- 1 T. oil
- ¾ cup sunflower seeds (optional)
- 1½ tsp. dried oregano
- 1 tsp. dried basil
- 1 dash powdered thyme
- 1 tsp. garlic powder
- salt to taste
- 2 15-oz. cans diced tomatoes
- 32 oz. spaghetti sauce (see page 205)

NUTRITIONAL ANALYSIS PER SERVING
Calories: 299
Fat: 10 grams
Cholesterol: 0 mg
Carbohydrates: 47 grams
Fiber: 7 grams
Protein: 9 grams
Sodium: 679 mg

Kitchen Tip

To CHOP means to cut into small pieces larger than ¼ inch. To DICE means to cut into small pieces, about ¼ inch. To MINCE means to make those pieces very fine (2 to 3 times smaller than diced).

Sauté the carrots, zucchini, pepper, onion, and fresh tomatoes in a deep saucepan with the oil for 5 minutes. Add the sunflower seeds and spices for the last minute of cooking. Add the canned tomatoes and spaghetti sauce, and simmer for 30 minutes.

This is tasty served over cooked pasta and garnished with grated Parmesan cheese.

Option: Place all ingredients in a slow cooker, and cook on low for 4 hours.

Cost per serving (1½ cups): 57¢

Broccoli Casserole

Serves 4
Preparation Time: 20 minutes
Cooking Time: 20 minutes

- 16 oz. frozen broccoli (chopped or crowns)
- 2 T. butter
- ¼ cup diced onion
- 1 clove garlic, pressed
- 2 T. flour
- 1 cup milk
- 3 oz. cream cheese
- ¼ cup grated cheddar cheese
- ½ tsp. sage
- ½ tsp. salt
- 1 egg, beaten
- ⅓ cup homemade bread crumbs (page 210) or cracker crumbs

NUTRITIONAL ANALYSIS PER SERVING	
Calories: 281	
Fat: 18 grams	
Cholesterol: 94 mg	
Carbohydrates: 21 grams	
Fiber: 4 grams	
Protein: 12 grams	
Sodium: 797 mg	

Cook the broccoli according to the package directions. Set aside.

In a large saucepan over medium heat, melt the butter. Add the onions and garlic and cook, while stirring, for 1 to 2 minutes. Stir in the flour and make a paste. Immediately add the milk and keep stirring as it cooks. Once it begins to thicken, add the cheeses, sage, and salt. Continue cooking and stirring until the cheese is melted, then remove from the heat. Add the broccoli to the pan and stir to mix in. Blend in the beaten egg.

Pour the mixture into a buttered 8x8 casserole dish. Sprinkle with bread crumbs. Bake at 350° for 20 minutes or until crumbs are dark brown.

Cost per serving (1¼ cups): 62¢

 *Kitchen Tip*

BROCCOLI is an excellent source of calcium. One cup of steamed broccoli contains 190 mg of calcium (one cup of skim milk has 300 mg). This recipe provides 95 mg of calcium per serving.

Tofu Eggless Salad

Serves 4
Preparation Time: 15 minutes

- ½ lb. tofu, drained and crumbled
- 2 green onions, finely chopped
- ¼ tsp. garlic powder
- 3 T. minced celery
- 1 T. prepared mustard
- 1½ tsp. soy sauce
- ¼ tsp. tumeric
- 1 T. sweet pickle relish
- 2 T. lowfat mayonnaise

NUTRITIONAL ANALYSIS PER SERVING
Calories: 100
Fat: 7 grams
Cholesterol: 5 mg
Carbohydrates: 4 grams
Fiber: 1 gram
Protein: 5 grams
Sodium: 160 mg

Mix all of the ingredients in a mixing bowl. Serve on bread just like an egg salad sandwich.

Store any unused portion covered in the refrigerator.

Cost per serving (½ cup): 38¢

Kitchen Tip

If you need to STORE TOFU, submerge it in fresh water and seal it in a container. This will keep it for a few days.

Favorite Veggie Burgers

Serves 8
Preparation Time: 25 minutes
Cooking Time: 10 minutes

This is the first of four vegetarian burger recipes that our family enjoys.

- ½ cup sunflower seeds
- ½ cup walnuts
- 2 cups homemade bread crumbs (see page 210)
- ½ cup cooked rice (brown is best)
- ½ cup water
- 1½ tsp. low-sodium soy sauce
- 1 tsp. Italian seasoning (see page 209)
- ¼ cup rolled oats
- 1 T. no-salt seasoning (e.g., Mrs. Dash, Spike)
- 1 tsp. garlic powder
- 1 tsp. cumin
- 4 egg whites
- 1 tsp. onion powder
- 1 T. dried parsley

NUTRITIONAL ANALYSIS PER SERVING	
Calories: 264	
Fat: 7 grams	
Cholesterol: 0 mg	
Carbohydrates: 39 grams	
Fiber: 3 grams	
Protein: 10 grams	
Sodium: 320 mg	

Kitchen Tip

Most recipes can be frozen in either the batter or cooked stage. Double this recipe and FREEZE the uncooked patties for a quick and inexpensive dinner in the future.

Place the sunflower seeds and walnuts in a blender; cover and blend until finely ground. You may need to stop the blender and stir the nuts around so all parts are blended.

Combine all of the ingredients in a mixing bowl. Mold into patties. If necessary, dust with flour to keep the shape. Fry in oil for 2 to 3 minutes per side or bake at 350° for 10 to 15 minutes or until the center is hot.

These are great served on hamburger buns with condiments.

Cost per serving (1 patty): 37¢

Seitan Supreme

Serves 8
Preparation Time: 15 minutes
Cooking Time: 40 minutes

Dough:

- 1 tsp. cumin
- 1 tsp. garlic powder
- 1 tsp. onion powder
- ½ tsp. ginger
- 1 cup vital gluten
- 1 cup water

Cooking broth:

- ½ cup soy sauce
- ¼ cup brown sugar
- 2 tsp. garlic powder
- 2 tsp. onion powder
- 2 qt. water

NUTRITIONAL ANALYSIS PER SERVING	
Calories: 29	
Fat: 0 grams	
Cholesterol: 0 mg	
Carbohydrates: 6 grams	
Fiber: 0 grams	
Protein: 13 grams	
Sodium: 881 mg	

Combine the spices for the dough and the vital gluten in a bowl. Stir well. Add the water and mix. It will be very sticky. Begin to mix the dough with your hands. Once all of the gluten is blended in, squeeze out any excess water. Shape the dough into a log (3-inch diameter), then slice into 1-inch pieces.

Place the cooking broth ingredients in a large kettle. Bring the water to a boil, and slip the slices of dough into the broth. Cover and simmer for 30 minutes. The "steaks" will expand to double in size.

Remove from the water. Your steaks are ready for cooking. They can be cooked in any way you would cook meat: coat with bread crumbs and

Kitchen Tip

VITAL GLUTEN is extracted from wheat, then dried and packaged. It is not to be confused with gluten flour. It is very high in protein. It can be found in the baking section in many grocery stores (it is added to bread dough to aid in rising) and in health food stores.

Seitan Supreme

(continued)

bake; barbecue them; fry them; add them to stews, curry, or chili; or slice and add to a sandwich. They only need to be cooked for a few minutes (3 to 5) to soften their texture. Any leftover steaks can be frozen at this stage or after final cooking. To make seitan gravy, fry some steaks in a lightly oiled skillet. After they have cooked, add ½ cup of the broth to the skillet and stir to make a gravy.

Cost per serving (6 oz.): 41¢

Tofu Burgers

Serves 4
Preparation Time: 15 minutes
Cooking Time: 10 minutes

- 1 lb. firm tofu
- ½ cup flour
- ¼ cup diced onion
- 2 garlic cloves, pressed
- 1 T. dried parsley
- 1 T. dried oregano
- 1 tsp. soy sauce
- 1 egg
- 1 T. oil

NUTRITIONAL ANALYSIS PER SERVING	
Calories: 200	
Fat: 10 grams	
Cholesterol: 45 mg	
Carbohydrates: 17 grams	
Fiber: 2 grams	
Protein: 13 grams	
Sodium: 556 mg	

Drain the water from the tofu package. Place all of the ingredients except the oil in a mixing bowl, and beat with a mixer until well blended.

Form into 4 patties about ½-inch thick. Heat the oil in a skillet on medium heat (use less oil if using a nonstick pan). Cook the patties for a few minutes on each side or until golden brown and firm. Serve on hamburger buns with condiments or teriyaki sauce (see page 200).

Variations: Try adding other seasonings to the mix such as sage, thyme, cayenne pepper, or teriyaki sauce.

Cost per serving (1 patty): 58¢

 Kitchen Tip

TOFU is a very good source of calcium. In ¼ pound of tofu (the amount in one patty in this recipe), there are 154 mg of calcium (there are 300 mg of calcium in 8 ounces of milk).

Lentil Burgers

Serves 6
Preparation Time: 40 minutes
Cooking Time: 10 minutes

- ½ cup dry lentils
- 1 large potato, grated finely
- ½ cup minced onion
- 2 garlic cloves, pressed
- 1 cup homemade bread crumbs (see page 210)
- 2 T. flour
- 1 egg
- ¼ tsp. prepared horseradish
- 2 T. low-sodium soy sauce
- ¼ tsp. salt
- ⅛ tsp. pepper

NUTRITIONAL ANALYSIS PER SERVING

Calories: 114

Fat: 1 gram

Cholesterol: 30 mg

Carbohydrates: 19 grams

Fiber: 6 grams

Protein: 7 grams

Sodium: 356 mg

Rinse lentils. In a covered medium saucepan, cook the lentils in 2 cups of water for 30 to 40 minutes or until tender. Drain well. In a large mixing bowl combine all of the remaining ingredients with the cooked lentils. Mix well. It will be moist but not thick.

Form into 6 patties (½ cup of mixture each) and fry in olive oil for 2 to 3 minutes per side or bake on a greased cookie sheet (400° for 10 minutes on each side or until golden brown).

Serve with a sauce (salsa, honey-mustard, orange-curry, etc.) or on a hamburger bun with condiments.

Store any leftovers in the freezer for up to several weeks.

Note: This can also be baked in a loaf pan and sliced like meatloaf.

Cost per serving (1 patty): 17¢

Kitchen Tip

If a recipe calls for EGGS, you can reduce the amount of cholesterol in the recipe by replacing one whole egg with two egg whites.

Black Bean Burgers

Serves 4
Preparation Time: 15 minutes
Cooking Time: 10 minutes

- 15-oz. can black beans
- 2 T. mayonnaise
- ¼ cup fresh cilantro, chopped
- 1 T. homemade bread crumbs (see page 210)
- ½ tsp. cumin
- ½ tsp. hot sauce (see page 204)
- 1 tsp. lime juice
- ½ tsp. onion powder
- ½ tsp. garlic powder

NUTRITIONAL ANALYSIS PER SERVING	
Calories: 182	
Fat: 6 grams	
Cholesterol: 4 mg	
Carbohydrates: 24 grams	
Fiber: 6 grams	
Protein: 9 grams	
Sodium: 532 mg	

Rinse and drain the beans and place in a mixing bowl. Add the mayonnaise, and mash the beans with a fork or potato masher. Add the rest of the ingredients and mix well. Form into patties. Spray a skillet with cooking oil spray, and fry the patties for 2 to 3 minutes on each side, or bake at 350° for 3 to 5 minutes per side.

Serve on hamburger buns with condiments.

Cost per serving (1 patty): 26¢

 Kitchen Tip

CILANTRO comes from the same plant as CORIANDER. The leaves are called *cilantro,* whereas the seeds are called *coriander*. Cilantro, also known as Chinese parsley, is commonly used in Chinese, Mexican, and Caribbean dishes.

Tofu Manicotti

Serves 6
Preparation Time: 25 minutes
Cooking Time: 20 minutes

- 8 oz. manicotti shells
- 16 oz. tofu, mashed
- 1 cup shredded mozzarella cheese
- 2 egg whites
- 1 T. flour
- 1 T. broth powder (see page 226)
- 2 tsp. onion powder
- 2 tsp. garlic powder
- ½ tsp. pepper
- 1 T. Italian seasoning (see page 209)
- 2 cups spaghetti sauce (see page 205)

NUTRITIONAL ANALYSIS PER SERVING
Calories: 311
Fat: 11 grams
Cholesterol: 20 mg
Carbohydrates: 35 grams
Fiber: 3 grams
Protein: 18 grams
Sodium: 250 mg

Cook the manicotti according to package directions. Rinse under cold water. Mash the tofu in a large mixing bowl with a fork or potato masher. Add the cheese, egg whites, flour, broth powder, and spices. Mix well. Place one shell in the palm of your hand so it won't tear, and fill it with tofu mixture. Place it in a 9x13 baking dish. Fill the remaining pasta in the same manner. If there is extra tofu filling, scatter it across the pasta in the pan. Pour the spaghetti sauce over the pasta, covering thoroughly. Bake at 350° for 20 minutes.

Serve with garlic bread or salad.

Cost per serving (1 cup): 73¢

Kitchen Tip

SPAGHETTI SAUCE, also called marinara sauce, is a highly seasoned tomato sauce used on pastas and in other dishes. It is easily made from fresh or stewed tomatoes, herbs, and spices. It is cheaper to make it yourself and tends to be more flavorful.

Veggie Burrito

Serves 5
Preparation Time: 20 minutes
Cooking Time: 20 minutes

- ½ cup chopped raw carrot
- ½ cup chopped raw broccoli
- ½ cup frozen corn, thawed
- ¼ cup diced onion
- ½ tsp. chili powder
- ¾ cup grated cheddar cheese
- 5 fat-free flour tortillas (taco size)
- 5 tsp. ranch dressing

Combine all of the vegetables, chili powder, and the cheese in a bowl and mix well. Spread 1 teaspoon of ranch dressing on each tortilla. Scoop ½ cup of the vegetable mixture onto each tortilla. Roll up the tortillas and place on an ungreased baking sheet. Cover the tortillas with foil. Bake at 350° for 10 minutes.

Cost per serving (1 burrito): 47¢

NUTRITIONAL ANALYSIS PER SERVING
Calories: 230
Fat: 9 grams
Cholesterol: 19 mg
Carbohydrates: 28 grams
Fiber: 2 grams
Protein: 9 grams
Sodium: 564 mg

Kitchen Tip

When a recipe calls for FRESH VEGETABLES, feel free to substitute your favorite vegetables for those listed. Most vegetables will work in most recipes.

Tofu Scampi

Serves 4
Preparation Time: 15 minutes
Cooking time: 10 minutes

- 1 lb. firm tofu
- 4 T. olive oil, divided
- ¼ cup cornstarch
- 5 cloves garlic, pressed
- 2 T. minced fresh basil
- 6 mushrooms, sliced
- 2 T. lemon juice

NUTRITIONAL ANALYSIS PER SERVING

Calories: 166

Fat: 13 grams

Cholesterol: 0 mg

Carbohydrates: 8 grams

Fiber: 1 gram

Protein: 7 grams

Sodium: 7 mg

Slice the tofu into 1-inch cubes. Pat dry with a paper towel. Place 2 tablespoons of the olive oil in a shallow dish. Place the cornstarch in a separate shallow dish. Toss the tofu in the oil, covering all sides, then roll in the cornstarch. Place the tofu pieces in one layer on a baking sheet. Bake at 400° for 10 minutes or until crispy.

Combine 2 tablespoons olive oil, the garlic, basil, and mushrooms in a shallow pan. Sauté on medium heat until the garlic is golden brown. Remove from heat. Stir in the lemon juice. Toss in the tofu.

Serve over a bed of braised spinach or fettuccine noodles.

Cost per serving (1 cup): 58¢

 Kitchen Tip

BRAISING is a cooking method in which food is first browned in a little oil, then covered and cooked over low heat in a small amount of liquid.

Meatless Shepherd's Pie

Serves 6
Preparation Time: 25 minutes
Cooking Time: 20 minutes

- 1 cup TVP granules
- ¼ cup broth powder (see page 226)
- 2½ cups hot water, divided
- ½ onion, diced
- 1 carrot, diced
- 1 celery rib, diced
- 3 T. flour
- 1 T. Worcestershire sauce
- 1 T. Italian seasoning (see page 209)
- ¼ tsp. pepper
- ½ cup grated cheddar cheese
- 3 cups mashed potatoes

NUTRITIONAL ANALYSIS PER SERVING	
Calories: 212	
Fat: 5 grams	
Cholesterol: 13 mg	
Carbohydrates: 30 grams	
Fiber: 4 grams	
Protein: 14 grams	
Sodium: 434 mg	

In a mixing bowl, combine the TVP, broth powder, 2 cups of the water, onion, carrot, and celery. Let rest for 15 minutes. Transfer to a large skillet and turn on low heat. In a small bowl, combine the flour, Worcestershire sauce, ½ cup water, and seasonings. Mix into a paste, and add to the TVP mixture. Simmer until it thickens, stirring constantly.

Spread the mixture evenly in a greased 2-qt. baking dish.

In a separate mixing bowl, combine the cheese with the mashed potatoes and mix well. Spread the mashed potatoes over the TVP mixture. Bake uncovered at 350° for 15 to 20 minutes or until the mashed potatoes are golden brown.

Option: Add 1 T. horseradish sauce to the potatoes for an extra zing.

Cost per serving (1 cup): 41¢

Kitchen Tip

A SHEPHERD'S PIE can be a combination of any vegetables and leftover meat. Be creative and substitute what you have on hand.

Cheese Soufflé

Serves 6
Preparation Time: 20 minutes
Cooking Time: 30 minutes

- 1½ cups low-fat milk
- ¼ cup flour
- 1½ cups grated cheddar cheese
- 1½ tsp. Dijon mustard
- ½ tsp. celery salt
- 5 eggs, separated
- ¼ tsp. cream of tartar

Grease a 2-qt. baking dish. Heat the milk and flour in a deep saucepan, stirring constantly until it thickens, about 5 minutes. Using a whisk is very helpful. Remove from heat and mix in cheese, mustard, and celery salt. Place the egg yolks in a separate bowl. Add 1 cup of the milk mixture to the yolks and mix well. Add the yolk mixture back into the milk mixture and mix well.

Place the egg whites and the cream of tartar in a clean bowl. Using a beater or whisk, beat the whites until foamy and stiff. Fold the egg whites into the yolk mixture. Pour into the baking dish. Bake at 400° for 30 minutes or until golden.

Option: Serve as a breakfast dish with fruit and muffins.

Cost per serving (¾ cup): 35¢

NUTRITIONAL ANALYSIS PER SERVING	
Calories: 213	
Fat: 14 grams	
Cholesterol: 183 mg	
Carbohydrates: 8 grams	
Fiber: 0 grams	
Protein: 14 grams	
Sodium: 400 mg	

Kitchen Tip

A WHISK is a cooking tool made from wire loops that makes blending easy. You whisk liquids in a circular motion. FOLD means to combine ingredients gently by turning the bottom portion of the mix onto the top. It is a delicate way of blending, often used with beaten and stiff egg whites to keep the air from being released.

Lentil Stew

Serves 6
Preparation Time: 20 minutes
Cooking Time: 40 minutes

- 1 cup dry lentils
- 6 cups water
- 2 T. broth powder (see page 226)
- 2 T. soy sauce
- 1 onion, diced
- 4 carrots, diced
- 2 celery stalks, diced
- 4 potatoes, diced
- ½ tsp. sage
- ½ tsp. dried parsley
- 3 T. flour
- 3 T. butter, melted

Rinse the lentils. Add all of the ingredients except the flour and butter to a large pot. Cook over medium heat for 35 minutes.

In a small bowl, mix the flour and butter into a paste. Whisk the paste into the stew and stir constantly for 3 to 4 minutes. The stew will thicken as you stir.

Serve alone or over polenta (see page 76).

Cost per serving (2 cups): 42¢

NUTRITIONAL ANALYSIS PER SERVING

Calories: 248

Fat: 6 grams

Cholesterol: 16 mg

Carbohydrates: 38 grams

Fiber: 13 grams

Protein: 12 grams

Sodium: 499 mg

Kitchen Tip

STEW is a general term for any food (meat, vegetables, fish) that is barely covered with a liquid, covered with a lid, and simmered slowly (or stewed). This method of cooking releases and mixes flavors as well as tenderizes meats and vegetables.

Sloppy Joes

Serves 4
Preparation Time: 10 minutes
Cooking Time: 10 minutes

- 1 cup TVP granules
- 1 cup hot water
- 2 cloves garlic, pressed
- ½ cup diced onion
- 6-oz. can tomato paste
- 1 tsp. Italian seasoning (see page 209)
- 1 T. Worcestershire sauce
- ¼ cup ketchup
- ½ tsp. celery salt
- ½ tsp. black pepper
- 4 hamburger buns

NUTRITIONAL ANALYSIS PER SERVING	
Calories: 253	
Fat: 3 grams	
Cholesterol: 0 mg	
Carbohydrates: 43 grams	
Fiber: 7 grams	
Protein: 18 grams	
Sodium: 730 mg	

Combine all of the ingredients (except the buns) in a large pot and whisk, mixing well. Simmer for 10 minutes or until the TVP granules are tender.

Toast the buns if desired. Scoop ¾ cup sauce onto each bun and serve immediately.

Cost per serving (1 sandwich): 32¢

Kitchen Tip

LYCOPENE, an antioxidant found in tomatoes and watermelon, has been shown to help reduce the risk of prostate cancer. Tomato sauce and tomato paste are excellent sources of lycopene since the tomato is concentrated, and it can be incorporated into many dishes.

Spinach Delight

Serves 6
Preparation Time: 15 minutes
Cooking Time: 50 minutes

- 2 egg whites
- 20 oz. frozen chopped spinach, thawed
- ¼ cup water
- 1 onion, diced
- 4 cloves garlic, pressed
- 1 tsp. broth powder (see page 226)
- ¾ cup grated cheddar cheese
- 2 T. flour
- ¼ tsp. pepper
- 2 whole eggs
- 1½ cups nonfat sour cream
- 1 cup homemade bread crumbs (see page 210)

Beat the egg whites until stiff, and set aside.

Squeeze the water out of the spinach and discard. In a skillet, combine the water, onion, garlic, and broth powder. Simmer until the onions are tender. Add the cheese, and stir until melted. Sprinkle the flour and pepper over the mixture and stir in. Transfer the mixture to a large mixing bowl. Stir in the spinach, eggs, egg whites, and sour cream, and mix well.

Sprinkle ½ cup of the bread crumbs evenly in the bottom of an 8x8 baking pan. Pour the spinach mixture over the bread crumbs. Sprinkle the other ½ cup bread crumbs over the spinach. Bake at 350° for 40 to 50 minutes or until the center is firm.

Option: Add sliced mushrooms for added flavor.

Cost per serving (⅔ cup): 82¢

NUTRITIONAL ANALYSIS PER SERVING	
Calories: 256	
Fat: 8 grams	
Cholesterol: 85 mg	
Carbohydrates: 31 grams	
Fiber: 4 grams	
Protein: 14 grams	
Sodium: 493 mg	

Kitchen Tip

Most VEGETARIANS follow one of three types of diets: VEGAN, LACTO vegetarian and LACTO-OVO vegetarian. Vegans avoid all animal products including eggs and dairy products. Lacto vegetarians limit meat products but do eat dairy products. Lacto-ovo vegetarians eat eggs as well as dairy products.

Jonni's Potatoes

Serves 4
Preparation Time: 15 minutes
Cooking Time: 15 minutes

- 1 cup TVP granules
- 1 T. ketchup
- 1 cup boiling water
- 2 T. oil
- 3 large potatoes, diced
- ½ onion, diced
- 2 cloves garlic, pressed
- ½ tsp. celery salt
- ½ cup grated cheddar cheese
- 1 large tomato, diced

NUTRITIONAL ANALYSIS PER SERVING	
Calories: 253	
Fat: 12 grams	
Cholesterol: 15 mg	
Carbohydrates: 22 grams	
Fiber: 6 grams	
Protein: 17 grams	
Sodium: 409 mg	

Combine the first 3 ingredients in a small mixing bowl. While that is soaking, heat the oil in a large skillet over medium heat. Add the potatoes and cook, stirring constantly, for 5 to 10 minutes, or until the potatoes are tender. Add the onions, garlic, and celery salt, and cook for 1 to 2 minutes or until the garlic is golden brown. Add the TVP, cheese, and tomatoes, and stir 1 to 2 minutes or until the cheese is melted and well distributed.

This is great served with a salad.

Cost per serving (1 cup): 45¢

Kitchen Tip

There are hundreds of varieties of POTATOES in the world. The RUSSET is long and has a brown skin. It is commonly used for baking and frying because of its low moisture and high starch content. The YUKON GOLD has a rich, buttery flavor and tender texture. RED potatoes are usually boiled because of their low starch and high moisture content. NEW POTATO is a term for any potato picked young (before the starch develops), making it crisp.

To prevent sprouting, put an apple in the bag with the potatoes.

Spanish Pie

Serves 6
Preparation Time: 15 minutes
Cooking Time: 20 minutes

- 1 cup TVP granules
- 1 cup boiling water
- 2 T. oil
- ½ onion, diced
- 2 cloves garlic, pressed
- 2 T. Mexican seasoning mix (see page 215)
- 6 oz. tomato sauce
- 1 cup grated cheddar cheese, divided
- ¾ cup cornmeal
- 1 T. sugar
- 1½ tsp. baking powder
- 2 egg whites
- ⅓ cup milk
- 4-oz. can diced green chilies

NUTRITIONAL ANALYSIS PER SERVING	
Calories: 268	
Fat: 11 grams	
Cholesterol: 20 mg	
Carbohydrates: 27 grams	
Fiber: 5 grams	
Protein: 16 grams	
Sodium: 630 mg	

In a small mixing bowl, combine the TVP and boiling water. While that soaks, heat the oil in a large skillet and cook the onions and garlic, stirring constantly, for 1 to 2 minutes or until the garlic is golden brown. Add the seasoning mix, tomato sauce, TVP, and half of the cheese to the onions. Stir 1 to 2 minutes or until the cheese is melted and well distributed, then remove the pan from the heat.

In a separate mixing bowl, combine the cornmeal, sugar, baking powder, egg whites, milk, green chilies, and the other half of the cheese. Mix until everything is moist, but don't overmix. Spread the TVP mixture evenly in an 8x8 baking dish. Pour the cornmeal mixture over the top and spread evenly. Bake at 425° for 20 minutes or until the corn bread is cooked through.

Cost per serving (1 cup): 50¢

Kitchen Tip

There are many variations of CORN BREAD. Try adding ¼ cup crumbled bacon, 1 T. molasses, or 2 T. scallions to your favorite recipe.

CHAPTER 8

The Twelve Days of Turkey

Whenever I see turkeys on sale I buy an extra-large one so we'll have leftovers. It's an inexpensive source of meat, and it's very tasty! But sometimes my family gets tired of turkey. That's when I must be creative with my leftover turkey.

I have provided several of our family's favorite turkey recipes for you to enjoy.

TURKEY SANDWICHES

One of the most common (and delicious!) ways to use leftover turkey is to make a turkey sandwich. But did you know that there are dozens of ways people make them? Here are some ideas to jazz up your next sandwich:

- Spread mayonnaise and a dash of cayenne pepper over a tortilla instead of on bread; add sliced tomatoes, onions, and lettuce, and roll up.
- Use ranch dressing instead of mayonnaise
- Add ½ teaspoon pesto paste to the mayonnaise
- Use bleu cheese dressing instead of mayonnaise
- Use watercress instead of lettuce
- Use sliced green onions instead of sliced onion
- Use Thousand Island dressing instead of mayonnaise, and replace the lettuce with sauerkraut (this is best on rye bread)
- Add sliced avocados
- Add diced canned green chilies
- Vary the type of bread: try pita, rye, or sourdough
- Add Dijon mustard to the mayonnaise
- Add thinly sliced cheese to the sandwich. Be creative: use provolone, Swiss, Brie, or cheddar cheese
- Make a grilled cheese and turkey sandwich
- Use coleslaw instead of the lettuce and mayonnaise
- Use cranberry sauce or stuffing instead of mayonnaise

Turkey Tetrazzini

Serves 5
Preparation Time: 10 minutes
Cooking Time: 15 minutes

- ½ lb. thin spaghetti (vermicelli), cooked
- 2 T. olive oil
- ¼ cup minced onion
- 3 cloves garlic, pressed
- 3 T. flour
- ¼ cup grated Parmesan cheese
- 2 cups water
- 1 cup milk
- 2 cups cooked, cubed turkey

NUTRITIONAL ANALYSIS PER SERVING
Calories: 336
Fat: 10 grams
Cholesterol: 35 mg
Carbohydrates: 40 grams
Fiber: 1 gram
Protein: 21 grams
Sodium: 162 mg

Cook spaghetti according to package directions; drain and set aside.

In a skillet, heat the oil over medium heat and brown the onion and garlic. Add the flour and Parmesan cheese to form a paste. Add the water and milk, and stir over the heat until thickened.

In a 9x13 baking dish, layer half of the turkey, followed by half of the spaghetti and half of the sauce. Repeat the layers, ending with the sauce on the top.

Bake for 15 minutes at 350°, or until heated through and golden brown.

Cost per serving (1¼ cups): 31¢

Kitchen Tip

A whole turkey should be cooked to an INTERNAL TEMPERATURE of 170°. To get an accurate reading, insert the thermometer into the breast meat, avoiding any contact with the bones.

Quick and Easy Pot Pie

Serves 4
Preparation Time: 20 minutes
Cooking Time: 30 minutes

Crust:

- 1¼ cups baking mix (see page 170)
- ½ cup milk
- 1 egg

Filling:

- 1½ cups cooked, cubed turkey
- ½ onion, diced
- 2 stalks celery, diced
- 1 cup frozen peas and carrots
- ¼ cup (or 1 pkg.) chicken gravy mix
- 1 cup milk

NUTRITIONAL ANALYSIS PER SERVING
Calories: 327
Fat: 8 grams
Cholesterol: 91 mg
Carbohydrates: 37 grams
Fiber: 2 grams
Protein: 25 grams
Sodium: 975 mg

For the crust, combine the baking mix, ½ cup milk, and egg in a mixing bowl. Mix well. Set aside.

In a saucepan, combine the filling ingredients. Heat and stir until the sauce thickens. Pour into a pie plate. Spread the crust mix over the turkey filling. Place the pie plate on a baking sheet, and bake at 375° for 25 to 30 minutes or until the crust is golden.

Cost per serving (1½ cups): 39¢

Kitchen Tip

STUFFING cooked inside the turkey carries a risk of food-borne illness, so make sure it is cooked thoroughly. Use the thermometer to check the stuffing's temperature. The stuffing should be at 165°. To avoid the growth of bacteria in stuffing, do not stuff the turkey with stuffing until you are ready to bake the bird. Or cook it separately from the turkey. To save time, make the dressing the day before and keep covered in the refrigerator until you are ready to bake the bird.

Turkey Chili

Serves 4
Preparation Time: 15 minutes
Cooking Time: 20 minutes

- 1 T. oil
- 1 onion, diced
- 3 cloves garlic, pressed
- 1½ tsp. chili powder
- ½ tsp. cayenne powder
- ½ tsp. black pepper
- 1 tsp. cumin
- 15-oz. can white beans, drained
- 4-oz. can diced green chilies
- 15-oz. can low-sodium chicken broth
- 2 cups cooked, cubed turkey
- 2 T. lemon juice

In a large 6-qt. saucepan, heat the oil over medium heat. Add the onions and garlic, and cook until the garlic is golden (2 to 3 minutes). Add the chili powder, cayenne powder, pepper, and cumin; stir. Add the beans, green chilies, broth, and turkey. Heat until simmering, and then remove from heat. Add lemon juice and stir well.

Cost per serving (1½ cups): 82¢

NUTRITIONAL ANALYSIS PER SERVING
Calories: 287
Fat: 5 grams
Cholesterol: 55 mg
Carbohydrates: 28 grams
Fiber: 7 grams
Protein: 35 grams
Sodium: 893 mg

Kitchen Tip

Before selecting your turkey at the store, decide if you want it pre-basted or all-natural. PRE-BASTED means the turkey has been bathed or injected with a solution of broth and seasonings to add moisture. It makes for a more tender turkey. Sometimes this solution contains preservatives and sodium. ALL-NATURAL means no ingredients have been added to the turkey. This does not mean the turkey is free of hormones or antibiotics.

Turkey Hash

Serves 4
Preparation Time: 20 minutes
Cooking Time: 25 minutes

- 3 medium potatoes, peeled and diced
- 2 carrots, diced
- 2 T. olive oil
- 1 medium onion, diced
- 1 stalk celery, diced
- ½ tsp. salt
- ½ tsp. pepper
- 2 cups cooked, cubed turkey
- 1 T. Italian seasoning (see page 209)
- ½ cup grated cheddar cheese

NUTRITIONAL ANALYSIS PER SERVING	
Calories: 297	
Fat: 13 grams	
Cholesterol: 70 mg	
Carbohydrates: 17 grams	
Fiber: 3 grams	
Protein: 28 grams	
Sodium: 578 mg	

Place the potatoes and carrots in a large (4-qt.) saucepan. Cover with water, bring to a boil, and then reduce heat to simmer. Simmer for 5 minutes. Remove from heat and drain off water.

In a skillet, heat the oil over medium heat; add the onions and celery. Stir constantly and cook until the onions are clear (about 5 minutes). Add the potatoes, carrots, salt, and pepper, and cook until the potatoes are browned, stirring constantly (about 10 minutes). Add the turkey, Italian seasoning, and cheese, and stir until cheese melts.

Cost per serving (1½ cups): 47¢

Kitchen Tip

To assure healthy LEFTOVER TURKEY:

- Refrigerate leftovers no longer than 2 hours after taking the turkey out of the oven.
- Store turkey in the refrigerator for 3 to 4 days, or in the freezer for 4 months.
- Store stuffing and gravy in the refrigerator for 1 to 2 days, or in the freezer for 1 month.
- Never mix stuffing or gravy with meat when storing since one spoils faster than the other.

Turkey Stir-Fry

Serves 4
Preparation Time: 20 minutes
Cooking Time: 10 minutes

- ¼ cup low-sodium soy sauce
- ½ tsp. powdered ginger (or 1 T. grated fresh ginger)
- 1 T. brown sugar
- 1 tsp. cornstarch
- ¾ cup water
- ¼ tsp. paprika
- 1 T. vinegar (any type)
- 1 T. olive oil
- ½ onion, chopped
- 3 cloves garlic, pressed
- 3 cups chopped vegetables (fresh broccoli, bell peppers, snow peas, etc.)
- 2 cups cooked, cubed turkey

NUTRITIONAL ANALYSIS PER SERVING	
Calories: 167	
Fat: 5 grams	
Cholesterol: 55 mg	
Carbohydrates: 7 grams	
Fiber: 1 gram	
Protein: 24 grams	
Sodium: 622 mg	

Combine soy sauce, ginger, brown sugar, cornstarch, water, paprika, and vinegar in a mixing bowl. Heat the oil over medium-high heat in a large skillet or wok. Add onions and garlic, and cook until the garlic is golden, stirring constantly. Add the vegetables and cook for 3 to 4 minutes, stirring constantly. Add the turkey and the sauce mix. Continue to stir while cooking, until the sauce has thickened. If the sauce gets too thick, add 2 tablespoons of water at a time and stir until the desired thickness is reached.

Serve with rice.

Cost per serving (1½ cups): 82¢

Kitchen Tip

When COOKING A WHOLE TURKEY (or other poultry), plan on ¾ pound of bird per person. A 12- to 14-pound turkey would feed 8 to 10 people, with plenty of leftovers for any of the turkey recipes.

Turkey Gumbo

Serves 6
Preparation Time: 15 minutes
Cooking Time: 50 minutes

- 1 T. oil
- ½ cup flour
- 4 cups water, divided
- 2 T. broth powder (see page 226)
- 1 cup cooked, cubed turkey
- 1 cup diced Polish sausage
- 2 carrots, diced
- 2 celery stalks, diced
- 1 onion, diced
- 14-oz. can stewed tomatoes
- ¼ cup ketchup
- ½ tsp. salt
- ½ tsp. pepper
- ½ tsp. Italian seasoning (see page 209)
- ¼ tsp. cayenne powder
- 10 oz. frozen sliced okra
- 1 cup uncooked rice

In a large (6-qt.) saucepan, heat the oil over medium heat. Add the flour and stir, forming a paste. Add ½ cup of water and broth powder. Stir while it cooks, until it thickens. Add the rest of the water and stir until it is well blended. Add the remaining ingredients and simmer, covered, for 30 to 40 minutes, or until the rice is tender.

Cost per serving (1½ cups): 76¢

NUTRITIONAL ANALYSIS PER SERVING

Calories: 390

Fat: 15 grams

Cholesterol: 46 mg

Carbohydrates: 46 grams

Fiber: 4 grams

Protein: 19 grams

Sodium: 921 mg

Kitchen Tip

THAW A FROZEN TURKEY in the refrigerator. Allow 24 hours for every 5 pounds of bird. That means that a 20-pound turkey would need 4 full days to thaw. Don't ever thaw at room temperature.

Turkey Curry

Serves 6
Preparation Time: 10 minutes
Cooking Time: 15 minutes

- 5 T. oil
- ½ onion, minced
- 6 T. flour
- 2 T. curry powder
- ½ tsp. salt
- 1 tsp. sugar
- ¼ tsp. powdered ginger
- 1 cup water
- 1 T. broth powder (see page 226)
- 2 cups milk
- 2 cups cooked, cubed turkey
- 1 cup diced apple
- 1 tsp. lemon juice

NUTRITIONAL ANALYSIS PER SERVING

Calories: 258	
Fat: 14 grams	
Cholesterol: 40 mg	
Carbohydrates: 16 grams	
Fiber: 2 grams	
Protein: 18 grams	
Sodium: 324 mg	

In a large (6-qt.) saucepan, heat the oil over medium heat. Add the onion, flour, curry powder, salt, sugar, and ginger. Stir into a paste. Add the water and broth powder. Stir and cook until it is well blended. Add the milk and turkey, and stir until it thickens. Remove from the heat and stir in the apple and lemon juice.

ROASTING A TURKEY breast-side down allows the juices to run into the breast and makes the meat more tender and juicy.

If desired, serve over brown rice.

Condiments that are tasty with curry:

chutney	raisins
peanuts	coconut
pineapple	hard-boiled eggs
sweet pickles	

Cost per serving (1 cup): 37¢

Turkey Waldorf Salad

Serves 6
Preparation Time: 15 minutes

- ½ tsp. lemon juice
- ½ cup low-fat mayonnaise
- 2 cups chopped cooked turkey
- 1 cup diced celery
- 1 cup raisins
- ½ cup chopped walnuts
- 1 green apple, peeled, cored, and diced
- salt and pepper to taste

In a small bowl, mix the lemon juice with the mayonnaise. In a larger mixing bowl, combine the rest of the ingredients. Add the mayonnaise mixture and toss until evenly distributed.

If desired, serve on a bed of lettuce and sprinkle with paprika for added color.

Cost per serving (1 cup): 46¢

NUTRITIONAL ANALYSIS PER SERVING
Calories: 239
Fat: 9 grams
Cholesterol: 37 mg
Carbohydrates: 25 grams
Fiber: 2 grams
Protein: 16 grams
Sodium: 206 mg

Kitchen Tip

The USDA recommends an oven temperature of no lower than 325° for ROASTING TURKEYS to assure that the internal temperature reaches 170°. Some chefs, however, suggest another method that reaches the same goal: Roast the bird at 350° for one hour, then reduce the temperature to 200° and cook until done (around 7 hours for a 12- to 14-pound bird).

Turkey Creole

Serves 5
Preparation Time: 10 minutes
Cooking Time: 20 minutes

- ¼ cup olive oil
- ½ cup chopped onion
- ½ cup chopped celery
- 1 clove garlic, pressed
- ¼ cup flour
- 28-oz. can stewed tomatoes
- 2 cups cooked, cubed turkey
- ½ tsp. Italian seasoning (see page 209)
- ¼ tsp. cayenne pepper
- 6-oz. can tomato paste

NUTRITIONAL ANALYSIS PER SERVING	
Calories: 270	
Fat: 13 grams	
Cholesterol: 44 mg	
Carbohydrates: 20 grams	
Fiber: 4 grams	
Protein: 21 grams	
Sodium: 408 mg	

Heat the oil over medium heat in a large skillet; add the onions, celery, and garlic. Cook for 2 to 3 minutes or until the garlic is golden brown. Add the flour. Stir to make a paste. Add the tomatoes and cook, while stirring, until thick. Add the rest of the ingredients, and cook 10 to 15 minutes, stirring constantly.

If desired, serve over rice or pasta. For an attractive dish, serve over orzo (a rice-shaped pasta).

Cost per serving (1½ cups): 59¢

Kitchen Tip

BASTING A TURKEY several times during roasting can make the skin chewy. Instead, baste it once during the last 20 minutes of cooking. For added flavor, rub an orange half over the skin during the basting time instead of using your regular sauce.

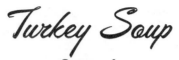

Turkey Soup

Serves 4
Preparation Time: 15 minutes
Cooking Time: 75 minutes

- turkey leg or part of carcass
- 6 cups of water
- 1 cup cooked, cubed turkey
- ½ cup chopped carrots
- ¼ cup chopped celery
- ¼ cup chopped onion
- 1 clove garlic, pressed
- 2 T. Italian seasoning (see page 209)
- 15-oz. can stewed tomatoes
- 1 cup uncooked rice
- 1 tsp. pepper
- ¼ cup broth powder (see page 226)

NUTRITIONAL ANALYSIS PER SERVING	
Calories: 264	
Fat: 1 gram	
Cholesterol: 27 mg	
Carbohydrates: 47 grams	
Fiber: 3 grams	
Protein: 16 grams	
Sodium: 277 mg	

Place the carcass with water in a large (6-qt.) pan. Add the remaining ingredients and place over medium-low heat. Let simmer uncovered for one hour.

When it is done, remove the carcass and pull off as much meat as you can, adding it back into the soup. Discard the carcass.

This is great with cheesy garlic biscuits (see page 171) to make a complete meal.

Cost per serving (1½ cups): 57¢

Kitchen Tip

Never boil a soup for a long time. EXCESS COOKING OF SOUP causes its flavor and body to fade. Cook it only as long as recommended.

Turkey Pie

Serves 6
Preparation Time: 15 minutes
Cooking Time: 25 minutes

- 2 T. olive oil
- ¼ cup chopped celery
- ¼ cup chopped onion
- 1 clove garlic, pressed
- ¼ cup flour
- 1 cup milk
- 2 cups cooked, cubed turkey
- 15-oz. can stewed tomatoes
- ½ cup grated cheddar cheese
- ½ tsp. Italian seasoning (see page 209)
- ½ tsp. salt
- ½ tsp. pepper

NUTRITIONAL ANALYSIS PER SERVING
Calories: 201
Fat: 9 grams
Cholesterol: 48 mg
Carbohydrates: 10 grams
Fiber: 1 gram
Protein: 20 grams
Sodium: 442 mg

In a large heavy skillet heat the oil over medium heat; add the celery, onions, and garlic. Cook for 2 to 3 minutes or until the garlic is golden brown. Add the flour. Stir to make a paste. Add the milk and cook, while stirring, until it thickens. Remove from heat and add the rest of the ingredients. Mix well.

Pour into a greased pie plate and bake at 350° for 20 to 25 minutes or until it is hot in the center.

Note: This recipe can be baked in a piecrust if desired. I omitted it because crusts are high in fat.

Cost per serving (1 cup): 41¢

Kitchen Tip

To PEEL GARLIC, try one of these techniques:
- heat the clove in the microwave for 15 seconds; then peel the skin right off;
- slap the flat side of the blade of a large wide knife over the clove;
- place the clove in a rubber tube and roll the clove while gently pressing.

CHAPTER 9

Slow Cooking

Slow cooking, also known as Crockpot cooking, is a great way to have a meal ready on a busy day. It's a wonderful tool for the frugal chef since it prevents us from ordering takeout on those busy nights. You can add the ingredients in the morning (or even the night before and store in the refrigerator), turn the pot on, and have a meal ready when you get home.

Since it uses a slow, steady, moist heat, the foods often come out tastier than if cooked in a traditional pan or oven. And the kitchen doesn't get hot! Foods can cook anywhere from 4 to 12 hours, making planning ahead easy. The cookers come in varying sizes, with some being large enough to cook whole chickens or even cakes.

NOTE: The recipes in this chapter are designed for a standard size slow cooker (3½ quarts). Do not double the recipes for larger slow cookers, as the times will not convert and the food will not cook correctly.

Fall-Off-the-Bone Beef

Serves 12
Preparation Time: 15 minutes
Cooking Time: 24 hours

- 1 cup water
- ½ cup soy sauce
- ½ cup brown sugar
- ¼ cup lemon juice
- 2 T. Worcestershire sauce
- ½ tsp. dried thyme
- ½ bunch fresh cilantro leaves, chopped
- 2½ lbs. chuck steak (or other inexpensive cut of meat), frozen

Combine all of the ingredients (except the meat) and pour in the bottom of the slow cooker. Place the meat in the sauce and cover. Cook on low for 24 hours. This slow cooking makes the meat fall off the bone.

Remove the meat from the juices and place on a cutting board. With two forks, pull the meat apart into shreds. It will take little to no effort at all. Drain any fat off of the juice and place the juice in a separate bowl.

Serve on French rolls with a cup of the juice on the side for an awesome French dip sandwich.

Cost per serving (5 oz.): 84¢

NUTRITIONAL ANALYSIS PER SERVING
Calories: 336
Fat: 18 grams
Cholesterol: 90 mg
Carbohydrates: 11 grams
Fiber: 0 grams
Protein: 31 grams
Sodium: 681 mg

 *Kitchen Tip*

Instead of serving CRACKERS with dip, serve TOASTED BREAD CHIPS. Slice a baguette (long, thin French bread loaf) into ½-inch slices. Lay them on a baking sheet. Lightly brush the tops (or spray) with olive oil. Sprinkle with seasoned salt and Parmesan cheese and bake at 300° for a few minutes until golden brown (watching closely so they don't burn).

Eggplant Parmigiana

Serves 6
Preparation Time: 20 minutes
Cooking Time: 2 to 3 hours

- 2 medium eggplants
- 1 egg
- 1 T. flour
- 1 T. water
- olive oil
- ¼ cup Parmesan cheese
- 1 T. seasoned bread crumbs (see page 210)
- 2 cups spaghetti sauce (see page 205)
- 2 cups (½ pound) sliced or grated mozzarella cheese

NUTRITIONAL ANALYSIS PER SERVING
Calories: 260
Fat: 15 grams
Cholesterol: 67 mg
Carbohydrates: 20 grams
Fiber: 6 grams
Protein: 13 grams
Sodium: 600 mg

Slice eggplant into ½-inch slices. Mix the egg, flour, and water in a bowl. Heat a little oil in a skillet. Dip the eggplant slices into the egg mixture, and fry until golden brown. Turn and cook the other side.

In a small bowl, combine the Parmesan cheese and the bread crumbs. Layer ¼ of the eggplant in the slow cooker. Sprinkle with ¼ of the bread crumb mixture, ¼ of the sauce, and ¼ of the cheese. Repeat the layering in the same order until all ingredients are used.

Cover and cook on low for 2 to 3 hours.

Cost per serving (1¼ cups): 58¢

Kitchen Tip

Use MEASURING SPOONS and not eating utensils for measuring ingredients. Eating utensils are not uniform in size.

Enchilada Casserole

Serves 6
Preparation Time: 20 minutes
Cooking Time: 4 hours

- 15-oz. can tomato sauce
- ½ cup water
- 2 tsp. hot sauce (see page 204)
- 5 fat-free flour tortillas (taco size)
- 1 cup grated cheese (cheddar or Monterey Jack)
- ½ onion, diced
- 1 lb. cooked lean ground beef

NUTRITIONAL ANALYSIS PER SERVING
Calories: 371
Fat: 19 grams
Cholesterol: 72 mg
Carbohydrates: 25 grams
Fiber: 2 grams
Protein: 23 grams
Sodium: 988 mg

Mix the tomato sauce, water, and hot sauce in a bowl. Pour half of the sauce mixture into a slow cooker. Layer a tortilla, ¼ of the cheese, then ¼ of the onions and meat in the cooker. Continue adding the layers until all of the cheese, onions, and meat are used. Top with a tortilla. Cover the tortilla with the other half of the tomato sauce mixture. Cover and cook on low for 4 hours.

If desired, serve with Spanish rice (see page 70), and add condiments such as cheese, sour cream, salsa, onions, etc.

Note: Substitute any type of meat (pork, chicken, etc.) or TVP.

Cost per serving (1 cup): 60¢

Kitchen Tip

For a quick, low-fat, low-cost SUB-STITUTE FOR SOUR CREAM, mix 1 teaspoon of lemon juice with 8 ounces of low-fat plain yogurt.

Chicken Taco Filling

Serves 4
Preparation Time: 5 minutes
Cooking Time: 6 to 8 hours

- 1 cup low-sodium chicken broth
- 1 packet taco seasoning mix or 3 T. Mexican seasoning mix (see page 215)
- 1 lb. boneless, skinless chicken breast

Pour the chicken broth into the slow cooker. Dissolve the seasoning mix in the broth. Place the chicken breast in the broth. Cover and cook on low for 6 to 8 hours.

After the chicken is cooked, use two forks to shred it into small pieces. Use in tacos, burritos, tostadas, nachos, etc.

This is great served with Spanish rice (page 70).

Note: Substitute any type of meat (pork, beef, etc.) or TVP.

Cost per serving (¼ lb.): 72¢

NUTRITIONAL ANALYSIS PER SERVING	
Calories: 139	
Fat: 2 grams	
Cholesterol: 66 mg	
Carbohydrates: 2 grams	
Fiber: 0 grams	
Protein: 30 grams	
Sodium: 239 mg	

Kitchen Tip

SLOW COOKING does not allow for much evaporation of natural juices in a recipe, so the end product will have more liquid in it. You may want to add more spices to the recipe to allow for this if you are using a regular recipe in a slow cooker.

Crock Lasagna

Serves 8
Preparation Time: 20 minutes
Cooking Time: 6 to 8 hours, or 3 to 4 hours

- 1 lb. cooked lean meat (ground beef, ground turkey, etc.)
- 1 onion, chopped
- 2 cloves garlic, pressed
- 12 oz. cottage cheese or ricotta
- 1 cup grated cheese (cheddar, Monterey Jack, or mozzarella)
- 12 oz. tomato paste
- 1½ cups water
- 2 T. dried basil
- 2 T. dried parsley
- 1½ tsp. salt
- ½ tsp. pepper
- 8 lasagna noodles (approx. one 10-oz. pkg.)

NUTRITIONAL ANALYSIS PER SERVING
Calories: 351
Fat: 21 grams
Cholesterol: 77 mg
Carbohydrates: 19 grams
Fiber: 3 grams
Protein: 21 grams
Sodium: 632 mg

In a bowl, combine everything except the noodles. Mix well. Spread 1 cup of the mix in the bottom of the slow cooker. Break up 3 of the noodles so they will fit in the slow cooker, and lay them over the sauce. Cover with 1 cup of sauce. Spread the sauce so the noodles are covered entirely. Break up 3 more noodles and lay them over the sauce. Cover these with 1 cup of sauce, making sure to cover each noodle entirely. Repeat the procedure one more time, using the last 2 noodles. Use all of the remaining sauce, making sure that each noodle is covered entirely.

Cover and cook on low for 6 to 8 hours or on high for 3 to 4 hours.

This is great served with garlic bread and a salad.

Cost per serving (1 cup): 90¢

Kitchen Tip

To AVOID TEARS WHILE CHOPPING ONIONS, freeze the onion for 30 minutes before chopping. Sulphur compounds in the onion cause the tearing. If you need only half an onion, you can STORE HALF: the half with the root attached will store longer.

Turkey Log

Serves 4
Preparation Time: 10 minutes
Cooking Time: 6 to 8 hours, or 3 to 4 hours

- 1 lb. frozen ground turkey log
- 3 potatoes
- 15-oz. can diced tomatoes
- 1 T. vinegar
- 1 T. Italian seasoning (see page 209)
- ½ tsp. onion powder
- ½ tsp. garlic powder

Place ground turkey log in the slow cooker. (If frozen tubes of ground turkey are not available in your area, form ground turkey into a 6-inch log.) Cut the potatoes in half and place the halves around the log.

In a bowl, mix the tomatoes with the vinegar and spices. Pour the mixture over the log and potatoes, moistening all parts.

Cover and cook on low for 6 to 8 hours or on high for 3 to 4 hours. If your ground turkey is thawed, cook on low for 3 to 4 hours or on high for 1 to 2 hours (or until done).

Cost per serving (¼ lb.): 52¢

**NUTRITIONAL ANALYSIS
PER SERVING**

Calories: 245

Fat: 10 grams

Cholesterol: 90 mg

Carbohydrates: 17 grams

Fiber: 2 grams

Protein: 22 grams

Sodium: 285 mg

Kitchen Tip

Buying spices in little bottles at the grocery store can be costly. Instead, buy them in bulk from health food stores or warehouse clubs. Save the little bottles from the grocery store and refill them from the larger containers. This could SAVE 75% ON SPICES.

Chicken Chile Verde

Serves 6
Preparation Time: 10 minutes
Cooking Time: 8 hours

- 1 lb. boneless, skinless chicken breasts (2 to 3 breasts)
- 4 oz. can diced green chilies
- 8 oz. sour cream
- 1 garlic clove, crushed
- ½ cup diced onion
- 3 oz. diced ripe olives
- ½ cup grated mozzarella cheese

Place the chicken and the rest of the ingredients in the slow cooker. Cover and cook on low for 8 hours.

Serve over rice. This is also good served on a tortilla.

Cost per serving (6 oz.): 89¢

NUTRITIONAL ANALYSIS PER SERVING
Calories: 158
Fat: 6 grams
Cholesterol: 59 mg
Carbohydrates: 4 grams
Fiber: 1 gram
Protein: 22 grams
Sodium: 317 mg

Kitchen Tip

MOZZARELLA CHEESE is made from cow's milk curd that has been kneaded until it reaches the cheese's famous texture. It is usually made from low-fat milk but can be made from whole or skim milk. It has a drier consistency than most cheeses and a very mild flavor.

Pull-Apart Chicken

Serves 4
Preparation Time: 10 minutes
Cooking Time: 8 to 10 hours

- ¾ lb. boneless, skinless chicken breasts (2 to 3 large)
- ½ cup water
- 1 tsp. vinegar
- ½ tsp. onion powder
- ½ tsp. garlic powder
- 1 tsp. Italian seasoning (see page 209)
- 1 tsp. sugar
- ½ tsp. celery salt
- 4 hamburger buns

NUTRITIONAL ANALYSIS PER SERVING	
Calories: 232	
Fat: 4 grams	
Cholesterol: 49 mg	
Carbohydrates: 25 grams	
Fiber: 0 grams	
Protein: 24 grams	
Sodium: 498 mg	

Place the chicken and the rest of the ingredients (except the hamburger buns) in the slow cooker. Cover and cook on low for 8 to 10 hours. During the last 2 hours of cooking, use a fork to break apart the chicken into strands. The longer it cooks, the easier this becomes.

Spoon over hamburger buns and serve. This is also good served on a tortilla.

Cost per serving (½ cup meat in a bun): 52¢

Kitchen Tip

Cooking meat at a LOW TEMPERATURE for a long period of time creates tender, moist meat that falls off the bone.

Lemon Chicken

Serves 4
Preparation Time: 10 minutes
Cooking Time: 4 to 5 hours

- 1 lb. or 4 small skinless chicken breasts
- 1 tsp. Italian seasoning (see page 209)
- 2 T. diced onion
- 2 cloves garlic, pressed
- ½ tsp. pepper
- 1½ T. lemon juice
- ¼ cup water

NUTRITIONAL ANALYSIS PER SERVING
Calories: 137
Fat: 2 grams
Cholesterol: 66 mg
Carbohydrates: 2 grams
Fiber: 0 grams
Protein: 26 grams
Sodium: 97 mg

Lay the chicken in the slow cooker, trying not to overlap too much. Sprinkle the Italian seasoning, onion, garlic, and pepper over the chicken. Pour the lemon juice and water on top.

Cover and cook on low for 4 to 5 hours.

Cost per serving (¼ lb.): 77¢

 Kitchen Tip

To get rid of the strong smell after chopping onion or garlic, rub the knife, cutting board, or even your hands with a fresh LEMON.

Teriyaki Chicken

Serves 4
Preparation Time: 10 minutes
Cooking Time: 6 to 8 hours, or 3 to 4 hours

- 2 T. water
- ¼ cup low-sodium soy sauce
- ½ tsp. ground ginger
- 2 T. diced onion
- 2 cloves garlic, pressed
- 2 tsp. brown sugar
- 1 lb. or 4 small skinless chicken breasts
- ½ onion, sliced
- 1 bell pepper, sliced

NUTRITIONAL ANALYSIS PER SERVING	
Calories: 154	
Fat: 2 grams	
Cholesterol: 66 mg	
Carbohydrates: 5 grams	
Fiber: 1 gram	
Protein: 28 grams	
Sodium: 630 mg	

In a small bowl, combine the water, soy sauce, ginger, onion, garlic, and brown sugar. Place the chicken in the slow cooker. Lay the sliced onion and bell pepper over the chicken. Pour the sauce over them.

Cover and cook on low for 6 to 8 hours or on high for 3 to 4 hours.

If desired, serve with rice.

Cost per serving (¼ lb.): 71¢

Kitchen Tip

SOY SAUCE is made from fermented soybeans, wheat, and barley. It is widely used in Chinese and Japanese cooking. It comes in dark, light, Chinese black, and tamari styles. Light soy sauce is usually saltiest of all and is thin. Be sure to read the label when you're buying soy sauce to make sure that "light" or "lite" means low-sodium. Dark soy sauce is thicker, darker, and less salty than light soy sauce. Chinese black soy sauce is very dark and thick because it has added molasses. Tamari soy sauce comes from Japan and is very similar to Chinese black soy sauce.

Black Bean Chili

Serves 4
Preparation Time: 10 minutes
Cooking Time: 10 hours

- ½ lb. cooked extra-lean ground beef
- ⅔ cup dry black beans, soaked and drained
- 8-oz. can tomato sauce
- 15-oz. can diced tomatoes
- 3 cloves garlic, crushed
- ½ tsp. ground cumin
- 2 tsp. chili powder
- ½ onion, diced
- 1 tsp. Italian seasoning (see page 209)
- ½ tsp. salt
- 1 cup water
- 1 tsp. lime juice
- 3 T. chopped cilantro

Combine all of the ingredients in the slow cooker. Stir, cover, and cook on high for 2 hours, then on low for 8 hours.

Note: Any type of dried bean can be used in this recipe.

This is great served with corn bread, and together they would make a complete protein.

Cost per serving (1½ cups): 60¢

NUTRITIONAL ANALYSIS PER SERVING	
Calories:	297
Fat:	11 grams
Cholesterol:	39 mg
Carbohydrates:	32 grams
Fiber:	8 grams
Protein:	120 grams
Sodium:	909 mg

Kitchen Tip

BLACK BEANS differ from pinto beans mainly in their flavor. The black bean is a bit sweeter than most other types of dried beans. If they are not available, pinto beans can be used instead.

Meatloaf

Serves 5
Preparation Time: 15 minutes
Cooking Time: 6 hours

Loaf:

- 1 lb. lean ground beef
- 1½ cups homemade bread crumbs (see page 210)
- 1 egg
- ½ cup low-fat milk
- 2 T. diced onion
- ½ tsp. salt
- 1½ tsp. Italian seasoning (see page 209)
- 2 T. ketchup
- 1 T. brown sugar

Topping:

- ¼ cup ketchup
- ¼ cup brown sugar
- ¼ tsp. prepared mustard

In a large mixing bowl combine the loaf ingredients and mix well. Shape into a loaf and place in the slow cooker.

Combine the topping ingredients in a small bowl. Pour over the loaf.

Option: Add chopped dill pickles or cheddar cheese to the mix before baking for a cheeseburger flavor.

Cover and cook on low for 6 hours.

Cost per serving (6 oz.): 42¢

NUTRITIONAL ANALYSIS PER SERVING
Calories: 327
Fat: 17 grams
Cholesterol: 100 mg
Carbohydrates: 22 grams
Fiber: 1 gram
Protein: 20 grams
Sodium: 545 mg

Kitchen Tip

When baking MEATLOAF in the oven, you can make individual servings by baking the meat in muffin tins. Reduce the cooking time to allow for the smaller sizes.

Fajitas

Serves 6 (makes 10 fajitas)
Preparation Time: 15 minutes
Cooking Time: 6 hours

- 1 lb. boneless skinless chicken
- 1 onion, thinly sliced
- 1 bell pepper, thinly sliced
- 2 cloves garlic, pressed
- 2 tsp. chili powder
- ½ tsp. cumin
- ¼ tsp. salt
- 1 T. lime juice
- 1 T. oil
- 10 fat-free flour tortillas (7-inch)

NUTRITIONAL ANALYSIS PER SERVING
Calories: 236
Fat: 4 grams
Cholesterol: 44 mg
Carbohydrates: 40 grams
Fiber: 3 grams
Protein: 25 grams
Sodium: 458 mg

Slice chicken into ½-inch strips. Place the chicken in the slow cooker. Top with the onions and peppers. In a small bowl, combine the garlic, chili powder, cumin, salt, lime juice, and oil. Pour over the onions and peppers.

Cover and cook on low for 6 hours.

Using a slotted spoon, serve a few pieces of chicken and vegetables on a flour tortilla. Wrap the tortilla around the contents and serve immediately.

Options: Serve with salsa, sour cream, grated cheese, refried beans, and/or guacamole to top the meat filling.

Cost per serving (1 to 2 fajitas): 68¢

Kitchen Tip

TORTILLAS are the daily bread of Mexico. It is an unleavened bread, meaning there is no leavening (i.e., yeast), and it does not rise before baking. They are made from flour (corn or wheat), lard, water, and salt, flattened into a large pancake shape, and cooked on a hot griddle.

Jerk Chicken

Serves 4
Preparation Time: 10 minutes
Cooking Time: 5 hours

- 6 green onions, cut in 1-inch pieces
- 2 T. chopped fresh ginger
- 2 cloves garlic, pressed
- 1 tsp. allspice
- 1 jalapeño pepper
- ½ tsp. salt
- 1 T. lime juice
- 1 tsp. oil
- 1 T. honey
- 1 tsp. black pepper
- 1 lb. or 4 small skinless chicken breasts

NUTRITIONAL ANALYSIS PER SERVING

Calories: 236

Fat: 4 grams

Cholesterol: 66 mg

Carbohydrates: 23 grams

Fiber: 6 grams

Protein: 31 grams

Sodium: 380 mg

In a blender combine all the ingredients except the chicken. Blend on high for 1 to 2 minutes or until a paste forms. Place the chicken in the slow cooker. Spread the sauce over the chicken.

Cover and cook on high for 1 hour, then on low for 4 hours. Stir once every hour.

If desired, serve over rice.

Cost per serving (¼ lb.): 78¢

 *Kitchen Tip*

JERK seasoning originated in the Caribbean. The combination of spices varies from chef to chef, but it usually includes hot peppers, cinnamon, allspice, cloves, ginger, garlic, and onions.

Honey Chicken

Serves 4
Preparation Time: 10 minutes
Cooking Time: 4 hours

- 1 lb. or 4 small skinless chicken breasts
- ¼ tsp. curry powder
- 1 tsp. cinnamon
- ½ cup diced onion
- 3 T. oil
- ¼ cup honey
- ½ cup chopped fresh parsley
- ¼ tsp. powdered ginger
- ¼ tsp. nutmeg
- 1 tsp. salt
- 1 tsp. pepper
- ¼ tsp. paprika
- ½ cup water

In a large mixing bowl, combine all of the ingredients. Toss well to coat the chicken evenly. Place the mixture in a slow cooker. Cover and cook on low for 4 hours.

If desired, serve over rice or orzo (rice-shaped pasta).

Cost per serving (¼ lb.): 77¢

NUTRITIONAL ANALYSIS PER SERVING
Calories: 313
Fat: 13 grams
Cholesterol: 66 mg
Carbohydrates: 23 grams
Fiber: 2 grams
Protein: 28 grams
Sodium: 719 mg

Kitchen Tip

CINNAMON comes from the inner bark of a tropical tree. The bark is peeled during the rainy season and then dried. It curls as it dries and is sold as sticks or ground into powder.

Orange Carrots

Serves 6
Preparation Time: 10 minutes
Cooking Time: 2 to 3 hours

- 3 cups carrots sliced ½-inch thick
- 1 cup hot water
- 2 T. butter, melted
- 3 T. orange marmalade
- ½ tsp. salt

Place the carrots in the slow cooker, evenly distributing them. In a mixing bowl, combine the water, butter, marmalade, and salt. Pour the mixture over the carrots.

Cover and cook on low for 2 to 3 hours.

Cost per serving (½ cup): 35¢

NUTRITIONAL ANALYSIS PER SERVING
Calories: 133
Fat: 6 grams
Cholesterol: 16 mg
Carbohydrates: 21 grams
Fiber: 3 grams
Protein: 1 grams
Sodium: 372 mg

Kitchen Tip

MARMALADE is a jam that includes the rind of the fruit. It adds a bitter taste to the jam.

Sweet Potatoes and Apples

Serves 6
Preparation Time: 20 minutes
Cooking Time: 6 hours

- 5 medium sweet potatoes, peeled
- 3 apples, peeled, cored, and sliced
- ¼ tsp. nutmeg
- ¼ tsp. cinnamon
- ¼ cup maple syrup
- 2 T. butter, melted

Slice the sweet potatoes into 1-inch slices. Lay them in the slow cooker, then layer the apple slices over them. In a small bowl, combine the spices, syrup, and butter. Drizzle over the apples and potatoes.

Cover and cook on low for 6 hours.

Option: Sprinkle with ¼ cup chopped nuts (pecans or walnuts) for the last 30 minutes of the cooking time.

Cost per serving (1 cup): 41¢

NUTRITIONAL ANALYSIS PER SERVING

Calories: 187

Fat: 4 grams

Cholesterol: 10 mg

Carbohydrates: 37 grams

Fiber: 4 grams

Protein: 1 gram

Sodium: 50 mg

Kitchen Tip

Don't replace butter with BUTTER SPREADS. Spreads have added water to replace some of the fat, which can cause a recipe to turn out poorly.

CHAPTER 10

Breads and Muffins

Baking Mix

(like Bisquick)

Makes 10 cups
Preparation Time: 15 minutes

- 8 cups flour
- 1¼ cups powdered milk
- ¼ cup baking powder
- 1 T. salt
- 2 cups shortening (don't use butter)

Combine all of the dry ingredients in a very large bowl and mix well.

Cut in the shortening until it looks like coarse cornmeal. Store in an airtight container in the cupboard. This does not need to be refrigerated.

NOTE: This can be used in any recipe where Bisquick is called for.

Cost per serving (1 cup): 21¢

NUTRITIONAL ANALYSIS PER SERVING	
Calories: 759	
Fat: 42 grams	
Cholesterol: 2 mg	
Carbohydrates: 82 grams	
Fiber: 3 grams	
Protein: 13 grams	
Sodium: 698 mg	

If you dislike ROLLING AND CUTTING BISCUIT DOUGH, drop the dough by heaping tablespoons onto the baking pan.

Cheesy Garlic Biscuits

Serves 6
Preparation Time: 10 minutes
Cooking Time: 10 minutes

- 2 cups baking mix (see page 170)
- ⅔ cup low-fat milk
- ½ cup grated cheddar cheese
- 2 T. butter, melted
- ¼ tsp. garlic powder

In a mixing bowl, combine all of the ingredients. Mix well. Drop golf-ball-sized spoonfuls onto an ungreased baking sheet.

Bake at 450° for 8 to 10 minutes or until light brown.

Cost per serving (2 biscuits): 30¢

NUTRITIONAL ANALYSIS PER SERVING
Calories: 336
Fat: 21 grams
Cholesterol: 22 mg
Carbohydrates: 29 grams
Fiber: 1 gram
Protein: 8 grams
Sodium: 343 mg

Kitchen Tip

Don't crowd items in the OVEN. It affects their cooking time and may cause them to cook unevenly.

Easy Refrigerator Rolls

Serves 24
Preparation Time: 15 minutes
Cooking Time: 15 minutes
Recipe donated by Kat Osten

- ¼ cup butter, softened
- ½ cup sugar
- 1½ tsp. salt
- 2 cups lukewarm water
- 4½ tsp. active yeast
- 1 egg
- 6 to 7 cups flour (bread flour is recommended)

NUTRITIONAL ANALYSIS PER SERVING	
Calories: 170	
Fat: 3 grams	
Cholesterol: 13 mg	
Carbohydrates: 32 grams	
Fiber: 1 gram	
Protein: 4 grams	
Sodium: 157 mg	

In a large mixing bowl, combine butter, sugar, salt, and water. Mix well until dissolved. Stir in the yeast. Mix in the egg and 3 cups of the flour. Combine well, and then add the remaining flour, ½ cup at a time. Stop adding flour once the dough can be easily handled and is not too sticky. You may not need all of the flour.

Form the dough into a round ball. Place in a greased bowl. Rub the top of the dough with oil and cover with plastic wrap. Lay a dampened towel (use warm water) over the plastic wrap. Place in the refrigerator until ready to use (up to one week). Punch the dough down when it reaches the top of the bowl (about 1 to 2 times per day) and re-wet the towel as needed to keep moist. Bring the dough to room temperature before using.

This dough can be used the same day you make it or over a week's time. If you want to use it the same day, do not put it in the refrigerator, but let it rise 3 to 4 times (every 30 to 40 minutes in a warm room), punching down between rises.

Kitchen Tip

BREAD FLOUR has added gluten and vitamin C, and has a finer texture. These variations from regular flour allow the dough to rise faster and also give the bread a lighter texture. Bread flour can be purchased at most grocery stores.

Easy Refrigerator Rolls

(continued)

The dough can be frozen for up to several months. Wrap airtight and freeze after the dough has risen and been punched down at least one time.

Refrigerator Roll Variations:

There are so many things you can do with easy refrigerator rolls.

- *Rolls:* Place three small balls of dough into each cup of a greased muffin tin. Cover with a damp paper towel. Let rise until double in size (20 to 40 minutes). Bake at 400° until golden brown, about 12 to 15 minutes.

- *Cinnamon Sticks:* Roll one-third of the dough into a rectangle about ¼-inch thick. Using a spatula, cover the dough with ¼ cup soft butter or margarine. In a bowl mix ½ cup sugar plus 2 tsp. cinnamon. Sprinkle dough generously with sugar mixture. Fold dough in half and press edges to seal. Cut into 1-inch-wide strips and twist. Bake at 400° for 8 to 11 minutes. Repeat for other two-thirds of dough, or freeze remaining dough.

  Top with a glaze made from 1 cup powdered sugar, ½ tsp. vanilla extract, and a few drops of milk. Add milk a few drops at a time and mix well before adding more to assure proper consistency.

- *Breadsticks:* Roll a third of the dough into a rectangle about ¼-inch thick. Brush dough with olive oil. Sprinkle with 1 to 2 crushed garlic cloves and 2 T. shredded mozzarella cheese. If desired, add Italian herbs to the garlic and cheese. Fold the dough in half and press the edges to seal. Cut into 1-inch-wide strips and twist. Bake at 400° for 8 to 11 minutes.

Cost per serving (1 roll): 9¢

English Muffins

Serves 8 to 10
Preparation Time: 1 hour
Cooking Time: 20 minutes

- 1 cup milk
- 1½ T. dry yeast
- 1 tsp. sugar
- ¼ cup butter, melted
- 2 cups flour
- 1 tsp. salt

Warm the milk to 105°. Stir in yeast and sugar until dissolved. Let rest for 5 minutes. Once froth develops, stir in the melted butter. Mix well.

In a separate bowl, combine the flour and salt. Add the liquid and mix well. Turn the dough onto a floured surface and knead for 5 to 10 minutes or until it becomes elastic. Cover and let rise in a warm (200°) oven until double in size (about 20 to 30 minutes).

Roll dough into a 10-inch log shape and cut with scissors into 8 to 10 pieces, each about 1½ inches thick. Shape each piece into a circle and place on a greased baking sheet. Cover and let rise in a warm oven for 20 to 30 minutes or until springy to the touch.

Place on a greased griddle or cast iron skillet over medium heat and cook for 5 to 8 minutes, or until golden brown on the bottom (watch closely to avoid burning). Flip the muffins over and cook the same way on the other side.

Cost per serving (1 muffin): 21¢

NUTRITIONAL ANALYSIS PER SERVING	
Calories: 153	
Fat: 6 grams	
Cholesterol: 16 mg	
Carbohydrates: 21 grams	
Fiber: 1 gram	
Protein: 4 grams	
Sodium: 273 mg	

Kitchen Tip

DOUGH RISES best at a warm room temperature (80°). The temperature that feels comfortable to you is what dough likes.

Bread Machine Whole Wheat Bread

Serves 8 (1 loaf)
Preparation Time: 10 minutes
Cooking Time: 2 hours
Recipe donated by Brynda Filkins

- 3 cups whole wheat flour
- ¾ cup oats
- 1¼ cups water
- 1½ T. brown sugar
- 1 T. oil
- 1½ tsp. salt
- 2 T. honey
- 2 tsp. yeast
- 2 tsp. dough enhancer (see page 216)

Put all of the ingredients (except 2 tablespoons of the water) in the bread machine in the order suggested by your bread machine manual. After the dough has begun to blend, if it is too stiff and forms a hard ball, add the remaining water 1 tablespoon at a time until the dough softens a bit.

Set the bread machine on "Basic 1½-pound loaf," and wait for the great aroma!

Tip: Remove the bread as soon as the machine indicates that it is done. The bread can get soggy if left in the machine too long.

Cost per serving (1 slice): 13¢

NUTRITIONAL ANALYSIS PER SERVING	
Calories: 260	
Fat: 4 grams	
Cholesterol: 1 mg	
Carbohydrates: 49 grams	
Fiber: 6 grams	
Protein: 9 grams	
Sodium: 409 mg	

Kitchen Tip

Save BREAD BAGS from purchased bread and use them for storing your homemade bread. STORE BREAD at room temperature or in the freezer. Avoid storing bread in the refrigerator, as this dries it out and reduces its "fluffiness."

Honey Whole Wheat Bread

Serves 96 (6 loaves)
Preparation Time: 1 to 2 hours
Cooking Time: 30 minutes

I find it easier to bake several loaves of bread at once and freeze them.
Here is my favorite recipe.

- 3 T. yeast
- 6½ cups warm water (95° to 115°)
- 1½ tsp. vitamin C powder (ascorbic acid)
- 1½ tsp. lecithin
- 1 cup oil
- 1 cup honey
- 2 T. salt
- 1 cup vital gluten
- 11 to 15 cups 100% whole wheat flour

NUTRITIONAL ANALYSIS PER SERVING	
Calories: 80	
Fat: 2 grams	
Cholesterol: 0 mg	
Carbohydrates: 13 grams	
Fiber: 2 grams	
Protein: 3 grams	
Sodium: 134 mg	

In a very large mixing bowl, combine the first seven ingredients. Mix well. Let the mix rest for 5 minutes. Add the gluten and mix well. With the mixer running, slowly add the flour to the dough, one cup at a time. Once the dough begins to pull cleanly away from the sides of the bowl, you have added enough. Adding too much flour will make the bread crumbly. You may use more or less than the 11 cups, depending on the flour, air temperature, etc. If you have a kneading function on your mixer, turn it on for 6 to 15 minutes, watching for an elastic consistency. If not, knead on a floured board for 20 minutes.

Form into 6 loaves and place in greased loaf pans. Cover and put in a warm area until doubled in size (20 to 40 minutes). Remove the upper oven racks and place pans on the lowest level. Bake at 325° for 30 minutes.

Cost per serving (1 slice): 7¢
Cost per loaf: 99¢

Kitchen Tip

If you need to INTERRUPT YOUR BREAD RISING, place the dough in the refrigerator. This slows the rising down as well as allows a better flavor and texture.

Whole Wheat Muffins

Serves 12
Preparation Time: 15 minutes
Cooking Time: 20 minutes

- 2 cups whole wheat flour
- 1 tsp. baking powder
- 1 tsp. baking soda
- ½ tsp. salt
- ½ cup maple syrup
- 1 cup water
- ½ cup oil
- 1 tsp. vanilla extract

In a large mixing bowl, combine the dry ingredients. Stir until well mixed. In a separate bowl, mix the wet ingredients. Add the wet ingredients to the dry. Mix until blended, but don't over mix. Pour into greased or paper-lined muffin tins. Bake at 375° for 20 minutes.

Note: For a nonfat version, replace the oil with ½ cup pureed fruit (unsweetened applesauce, mashed bananas, prunes, etc.).

These are great served with raspberry butter (see page 196).

Cost per serving (1 muffin): 11¢

NUTRITIONAL ANALYSIS PER SERVING	
Calories: 184	
Fat: 10 grams	
Cholesterol: 0 mg	
Carbohydrates: 24 grams	
Fiber: 2 grams	
Protein: 3 grams	
Sodium: 227 mg	

Kitchen Tip

WHOLE WHEAT FLOUR has more nutrients than white flour: 91% more phosphorous, 86% more vitamin E, 85% more magnesium, 81% more vitamin B_3, 77% more vitamin B_1, 72% more vitamin B_6, 67% more vitamin B_2, 62% more zinc, and 89% more fiber.

Blueberry Muffins

Serves 16
Preparation Time: 20 minutes
Cooking Time: 20 minutes

- 2 cups flour
- ⅔ cup sugar
- 1 T. baking powder
- ½ tsp. salt
- ¼ tsp. ground nutmeg
- 1 cup milk
- 4 egg whites
- ⅓ cup butter, melted
- 1 tsp. vanilla extract
- 1½ cups blueberries (fresh or frozen)

NUTRITIONAL ANALYSIS PER SERVING	
Calories: 142	
Fat: 5 grams	
Cholesterol: 0 mg	
Carbohydrates: 22 grams	
Fiber: 1 gram	
Protein: 3 grams	
Sodium: 150 mg	

In a large mixing bowl, combine the dry ingredients. Stir until well mixed. In a separate bowl, mix the wet ingredients except the blueberries. Add the wet ingredients to the dry. Mix until blended, but be careful not to over mix. Add the blueberries and fold twice, just to distribute berries.

Pour into paper-lined muffin tins, filling them ⅔ full. Sprinkle the top of each muffin with a little sugar. Bake at 400° for 20 minutes. Let the muffins cool completely to ease removal from the paper liners.

Note: For a nonfat version, replace the butter with ⅓ cup pureed fruit (unsweetened applesauce, mashed bananas, prunes, etc.) and use nonfat milk.

Cost per serving (1 muffin): 16¢

 Kitchen Tip

When using FROZEN FRUIT in muffins or other baked goods, rinse it, and then pat it dry for even mixing and to avoid adding unneeded moisture to the batter.

Ultra Chocolate Muffins

Serves 12
Preparation Time: 15 minutes
Cooking Time: 20 minutes
Recipe donated by Kat Osten

- 1½ cups flour
- ½ cup sugar
- ¼ cup unsweetened cocoa powder
- 1 tsp. baking soda
- ½ tsp. salt
- ½ cup apple juice
- ¼ cup water
- ¼ cup butter, melted
- 1 T. vinegar (any type)
- 1 tsp. vanilla extract
- ½ cup chocolate chips

NUTRITIONAL ANALYSIS PER SERVING	
Calories: 168	
Fat: 6 grams	
Cholesterol: 10 mg	
Carbohydrates: 27 grams	
Fiber: 1.5 grams	
Protein: 2 grams	
Sodium: 235 mg	

In a large mixing bowl, combine the dry ingredients. Stir until well mixed. In a separate bowl, mix the wet ingredients. Mix well. Add the wet ingredients to the dry, and add the chocolate chips. Mix until blended, but be careful not to over mix.

Pour into greased or paper-lined muffin tins. Bake at 375° for 18 minutes.

Cost per serving (1 muffin): 13¢

Kitchen Tip

Tips for making FLUFFY MUFFINS:

- Do not over mix the batter—it should be lumpy. Over mixing releases gluten, which makes the muffin tougher.
- To form better peaks, heat the oven to 400° and bake for 5 minutes, and then reduce the heat to 375° for the remainder of the baking time.
- Always use fresh baking powder and soda.
- To add a better flavor, use apple juice instead of water.

Oat Bran Muffins

Serves 12
Preparation Time: 15 minutes
Cooking Time: 15 minutes

- 2¼ cups oat bran
- ½ tsp. salt
- 1½ tsp. cinnamon
- 1 T. baking powder
- 1 tsp. baking soda
- ¼ tsp. vinegar
- 1¼ cups low-fat milk
- 2 egg whites
- ¼ cup honey
- 2 T. oil
- 2 tsp. vanilla extract

NUTRITIONAL ANALYSIS PER SERVING	
Calories: 105	
Fat: 4 grams	
Cholesterol: 1 mg	
Carbohydrates: 21 grams	
Fiber: 3 grams	
Protein: 5 grams	
Sodium: 303 mg	

In a large mixing bowl, combine the dry ingredients. In a separate bowl blend the wet ingredients. Add the wet ingredients to the dry. Mix until blended, but don't over mix—it should be lumpy. Pour into greased or paper-lined muffin tins, filling them ¾ full. Bake at 425° for 12 to 15 minutes or until golden brown.

Option: Add ½ cup diced fruit (apples, peaches, berries, banana, raisins, etc.) with the wet ingredients for a tasty variation.

Cost per serving (1 muffin): 21¢

Kitchen Tip

OAT BRAN has been proven to reduce cholesterol. The body produces bile, which has cholesterol in it. The bile is reabsorbed by the body if not used. Oat bran binds with the bile in digestion and eliminates it before the body can absorb it. My husband ate 3 muffins per day and saw his cholesterol drop. Oat bran is sold in bulk at health food stores or in boxes in the hot cereal section of grocery stores. It is not to be confused with oats or oatmeal.

Easy Donut Holes

Serves 6
Preparation Time: 10 minutes
Cooking Time: 5 minutes

Donut holes:

- 1 can biscuit dough (8 biscuits)
- 1 to 2 cups oil

Glaze:

- 2 cups powdered sugar
- 1 T. vanilla extract
- ¼ tsp. nutmeg
- 3 T. milk

Blend all the glaze ingredients together with a spoon until smooth. Set aside.

Lay the biscuits on a cutting board and cut each biscuit into 4 pieces. Pour vegetable oil into a small saucepan so there is 1 to 2 inches of oil in the pan. Heat oil to 350° (medium heat).

Deep-fry the biscuit pieces until golden brown (only a few seconds on each side). Remove with a slotted spoon. Drain on paper towels. While they're still warm, dip the donut balls into the glaze.

For chocolate glaze, melt 1 cup chocolate chips in microwave for 30 to 60 seconds, stirring often (don't cook too long or they get hard). Stir into the glaze recipe above, and dip as directed.

Variation: Instead of cutting the biscuit into fourths, cut a small hole in the center (use a water bottle cap to do this), and fry the ring like a donut and the center like a donut hole.

Cost per serving (5 donut holes): 16¢

NUTRITIONAL ANALYSIS PER SERVING	
Calories: 348	
Fat: 20 grams	
Cholesterol: 1 mg	
Carbohydrates: 44 grams	
Fiber: 0 grams	
Protein: 1 grams	
Sodium: 88 mg	

Kitchen Tip

To cool or dry a dipped or GLAZED ITEM, it is best to lay it on a cooling rack. This allows air to freely flow around the food, making cooling quicker and preventing moisture buildup on the bottom of the pastry.

Corn Bread Cake

Serves 15
Preparation Time: 5 minutes
Cooking Time: 20 minutes

- 8.5-oz. box Jiffy corn muffin mix
- 9-oz. box Jiffy yellow cake mix
- 4 egg whites (or 2 eggs)
- ½ cup milk
- ¼ cup water

Combine all of the ingredients in a large mixing bowl. Whisk together until well blended, but don't over mix.

Pour into a greased 9x13 pan. Evenly distribute the batter in the pan. Bake at 400° for 15–20 minutes or until a toothpick or knife passes the "toothpick test."

Serve with honey butter (see page 195).

Note: This recipe can be baked into muffins if you prefer. Line muffin tins with paper liners. Fill them half full. Bake at 400° for 10 to 15 minutes, or until they test done with a toothpick.

Cost per serving (2-inch square): 13¢

NUTRITIONAL ANALYSIS PER SERVING

Calories: 150

Fat: 3 grams

Cholesterol: 0 mg

Carbohydrates: 27 grams

Fiber: 1 gram

Protein: 3 grams

Sodium: 276 mg

 *Kitchen Tip*

To test if a cake is done, do the TOOTHPICK TEST. Insert a clean toothpick into the center of the cake and pull it straight out. If any dough has stuck to the toothpick, it isn't done. The toothpick will be clean when the cake is done.

Fat-Free Zucchini Bread

Serves 24 (2 loaves)
Preparation Time: 10 minutes
Cooking Time: 60 minutes

- 3 eggs
- 1⅔ cups sugar
- 2 tsp. vanilla
- 1 cup unsweetened applesauce
- 2 cups grated zucchini
- 3 cups flour
- 1 tsp. baking powder
- 1 tsp. baking soda
- 1 tsp. salt
- 1 tsp. nutmeg
- 2 tsp. cinnamon

Combine the eggs, sugar, vanilla, and applesauce in a large mixing bowl. Whisk together until well blended. Stir in the zucchini. In a separate bowl, mix together the rest of the ingredients. Stir the flour mixture into the egg mixture, and mix well.

Pour into two greased 9x4 loaf pans. Evenly distribute the dough in pans. Bake at 350° for 50 to 60 minutes, or until a toothpick or knife comes out clean when inserted in the center.

Options: Add ¾ cup chopped walnuts, 1 cup chocolate chips, and/or 1 cup raisins with the zucchini.

* Each slice contains less than 1 gram of fat, so it is listed as zero. For a completely fat-free version, replace the 3 whole eggs with 6 egg whites.

Cost per serving (1 slice): 13¢

NUTRITIONAL ANALYSIS PER SERVING

Calories: 129

Fat: 0 grams*

Cholesterol: 23 mg

Carbohydrates: 28 grams

Fiber: 1 gram

Protein: 2 grams

Sodium: 164 mg

Kitchen Tip

There's always plenty of ZUC-CHINI at harvest time. If you have extra:

· Hollow out the center and stuff with bread stuffing.

· Toss 1 cup of shredded zucchini in with a coleslaw recipe.

· Add small chunks to a salsa recipe.

· Grill thick slices on the barbeque.

· Layer slices in a lasagna recipe.

Herb and Cheese Bread

(for bread machine)

Serves 8 (1 loaf)
Preparation Time: 10 minutes
Cooking Time: 2 hours

- 3¾ cups white flour
- 1¼ cups water
- 2 T. oil
- 1 tsp. salt
- 2 tsp. yeast
- 1 tsp. dough enhancer, optional (see page 216)
- 1 cup shredded cheddar cheese (sharp cheese tastes best)
- 2 T. dried minced onion
- 2 T. salt-free seasoning (see page 212)

NUTRITIONAL ANALYSIS PER SERVING
Calories: 255
Fat: 4 grams
Cholesterol: 1 mg
Carbohydrates: 47 grams
Fiber: 2 grams
Protein: 7 grams
Sodium: 272 mg

Put all of the ingredients except 2 tablespoons of the water in the bread machine in the order suggested by your bread machine manual. After the dough has begun to blend, if it becomes too stiff and forms a hard ball, add the remaining water 1 tablespoon at a time until the dough softens a bit.

Set the bread machine on "Basic 1½-pound loaf," and wait for the great aroma!

Tip: Remove the bread as soon as the machine indicates that it is done. The bread can get soggy if left in the machine too long.

Cost per serving (1 slice): 16¢

Kitchen Tip

CHEDDAR CHEESE comes in several types, including sharp and mild. The difference is in the aging time. The longer the cheese has aged, the stronger, or sharper, its taste. The yellow color is added during processing and has nothing to do with aging time.

Focaccia Bread

(for bread machine)

Serves 12
Preparation Time: 60 minutes
Cooking Time: 20 minutes

- 3½ cups white flour
- 1¼ cups water
- 4 T. oil, divided
- 1¾ tsp. salt, divided
- 2 tsp. yeast
- 1 tsp. dough enhancer, optional (see page 216)
- 2 tsp. whole rosemary sprigs

Put the first 6 ingredients in the bread machine, but keep out 2 tablespoons of the water, 2 tablespoons of the oil, and ½ teaspoon of the salt. Set the bread machine on "dough," and let knead for 10 minutes. After the dough has begun to blend, if it becomes too stiff and forms a hard ball, add the remaining 2 tablespoons water 1 tablespoon at a time until the dough softens.

Remove the dough from the bread machine, cover it with a damp towel or plastic wrap, and let it rest for 15 minutes at room temperature.

Uncover and knead 2 to 3 times. Grease a 9x13 pan and roll or stretch the dough out to fit the pan. Brush the dough with the remaining 2 tablespoons of oil. Cut the sprigs of rosemary so they are ¼-inch long, and scatter evenly over the dough. Sprinkle the remaining ½ teaspoon salt over the dough. Cover with a towel and let rise for 30 minutes.

Remove the towel after rising and press your finger into the dough every 2 to 3 inches to make impressions. Bake uncovered at 425° for 18 to 20 minutes.

Variations: This is excellent served with pesto sauce (see page 206). It also makes a delicious sandwich bread.

Cost per serving (4-inch square): 10¢

NUTRITIONAL ANALYSIS PER SERVING	
Calories: 268	
Fat: 8 grams	
Cholesterol: 1 mg	
Carbohydrates: 43 grams	
Fiber: 2 grams	
Protein: 6 grams	
Sodium: 472 mg	

Kitchen Tip

You can MEASURE GRANULATED YEAST in either ounces or teaspoons and tablespoons. One tablespoon of granulated yeast equals ½ ounce.

Pumpkin Bread

Serves 12 (1 loaf)
Preparation Time: 15 minutes
Cooking Time: 50 minutes

- 15-oz. can pumpkin
- ¼ cup maple syrup
- 1 egg
- 2 T. oil
- 1 tsp. vanilla extract
- 1½ cups flour
- ½ cup brown sugar, firmly packed
- 1 tsp. baking powder
- 1 tsp. baking soda
- ½ tsp. cinnamon
- ½ tsp. salt
- ¼ tsp. ground cloves
- ½ tsp. allspice

NUTRITIONAL ANALYSIS PER SERVING	
Calories: 162	
Fat: 4 grams	
Cholesterol: 18 mg	
Carbohydrates: 31 grams	
Fiber: 2 grams	
Protein: 3 grams	
Sodium: 281 mg	

Kitchen Tip

To accurately MEASURE DRY INGREDIENTS, fill the measuring cup to overflowing with a spoon. Then level off the top with a knife or spatula.

Place the pumpkin, syrup, egg, oil, and vanilla in a large mixing bowl and mix to blend, but don't over mix. In a separate mixing bowl, blend together the rest of the ingredients. Add the dry ingredients to the pumpkin mixture, and mix until blended.

Pour into a greased 9x4 loaf pan. Bake at 350° for 50 minutes or until a toothpick tests clean in the center. Remove the bread from the oven. Let cool for 10 to 15 minutes, then remove bread from the pan and put it on a cooling rack. Let cool completely before slicing.

Options: Add ⅓ cup raisins and/or ⅓ cup chocolate chips to the pumpkin mixture for added flavor.

Cost per serving (1 slice): 9¢

Blender Muffins

Serves 12
Preparation Time: 5 minutes
Cooking Time: 25 minutes

- 1½ cups milk
- 1¼ cups wheat berries
- ¼ cup oil
- ½ cup honey
- ½ tsp. vanilla
- 1 egg
- 1½ cups bran cereal (e.g., All-Bran)
- 1 T. baking powder
- ¼ tsp. salt

NUTRITIONAL ANALYSIS PER SERVING

Calories:	159
Fat:	5 grams
Cholesterol:	15 mg
Carbohydrates:	29 grams
Fiber:	6 grams
Protein:	4 grams
Sodium:	205 mg

Place the milk, wheat berries, oil, and honey in a blender; cover and blend on high for 3 to 4 minutes or until smooth. Stop the blender and add the vanilla and egg. Blend for 2 to 3 seconds. Add the cereal, baking powder, and salt. Cover and blend again for 5 seconds or until well mixed.

Pour into greased or paper-lined muffin tins. Fill ⅔ full. Bake at 400° for 20 to 25 minutes or until golden brown.

Option: For a tasty addition, add ½ cup fruit to the batter (banana, berries, raisins, etc.) when you add the egg.

Cost per serving (1 muffin): 21¢

Kitchen Tip

WHEAT BERRIES are sold in health food stores. There are two types: winter wheat and pastry berries. Winter wheat berries come in a variety of types, including red, hard, and white. They vary a bit in flavor, but are all used for yeast bread recipes, as they have gluten. Pastry berries do not have gluten and can only be used in recipes that call for baking powder or soda and eggs to raise the bread. For this recipe, pastry berries work best.

Orange-Cranberry Bread

Serves 12 (1 loaf)
Preparation Time: 20 minutes
Cooking Time: 50 minutes

- 1 orange
- 1 cup flour
- ½ cup oats
- ½ cup brown sugar
- 2 tsp. baking powder
- ½ tsp. baking soda
- ¼ tsp. nutmeg
- ½ tsp. cinnamon
- ¾ tsp. salt
- 1 egg
- 3 T. oil
- 3 T. water
- 1 tsp. vanilla extract
- ¾ cup fresh cranberries

NUTRITIONAL ANALYSIS PER SERVING	
Calories: 258	
Fat: 9 grams	
Cholesterol: 30 mg	
Carbohydrates: 40 grams	
Fiber: 2 grams	
Protein: 6 grams	
Sodium: 507 mg	

Wash the orange. Grate 2 teaspoons of the rind (zest) into a small bowl, and set aside. Cut the orange in half and squeeze ¼ cup juice from the orange; set aside (if it is less than ¼ cup, add water to make it ¼ cup). Cut out as much fruit from the orange as you can, and chop it into small pieces; set aside.

In a large mixing bowl blend together the flour, oats, brown sugar, baking powder, baking soda, nutmeg, cinnamon, and salt. In a separate bowl combine the egg, oil, water, orange juice, and vanilla. Add the orange pieces, orange rind, and cranberries. Mix well, and then blend in with the dry ingredients. Pour into a greased 9x4 loaf pan. Bake at 350° for 40 to 50 minutes, or until a toothpick tests clean in the center.

Options: Add ⅓ cup chopped walnuts or pecans to the dough before baking for added flavor.

Cost per serving (1 slice): 19¢

Kitchen Tip

REMOVING FAT from baked goods can make them dry. That is why it works best to replace the fat with a moist ingredient such as mashed or pureed fruit (applesauce, mashed banana, canned pumpkin, etc.).

Biscotti

Serves 18
Preparation Time: 20 minutes
Cooking Time: 40 minutes

- 4 cups flour
- 1½ cups sugar
- ½ tsp. salt
- 2 tsp. baking powder
- ⅓ cup butter
- ¼ cup shortening
- 4 eggs
- 1 tsp. vanilla
- 1 tsp. almond extract

NUTRITIONAL ANALYSIS PER SERVING
Calories: 233
Fat: 7 grams
Cholesterol: 49 mg
Carbohydrates: 38 grams
Fiber: 1 gram
Protein: 4 grams
Sodium: 176 mg

In a large mixing bowl, mix all of the dry ingredients. Cut in the butter and shortening until the dough is crumbly. In a separate bowl, combine the eggs and extracts. Add them to the dry ingredients and mix. Turn the dough out onto a floured surface, and knead for several minutes, until it is not sticking to the board.

Divide dough into 6 equal sections and roll them out to 8 inches long and several inches wide. Place the lengths on a greased baking sheet. Press them so they are 1 inch thick. Bake at 325° for 25 to 30 minutes.

Remove from the oven and slice into 1-inch-wide strips while the loaf is still warm. Lay the pieces on the same baking sheet and bake at 375° for 5 minutes. Turn the slices over and bake another 5 minutes. Store in an airtight container.

Options: Add ½ cup dried fruit, ground almonds, or chocolate chips to the dough. If desired, dip the biscotti in melted chocolate (these make nice gifts).

Cost per serving (1 biscotti): 8¢

Kitchen Tip

The TYPE OF PAN you bake anything on can affect the outcome of the recipe. Shiny pans work best. The dark or nonstick pans cook hotter, so it's best to reduce the oven temperature by 25 degrees.

CHAPTER 11

Sauces and Dressings

Caesar Dressing

Makes 1¼ cups (10 servings)
Preparation Time: 10 minutes

- ½ cup grated Parmesan cheese
- ½ cup olive oil
- ¼ cup lemon juice
- 2 cloves garlic
- 1 tsp. Worcestershire sauce

Place all of the ingredients in a blender, cover, and blend until smooth.

Store in an airtight container in the refrigerator and this should last for several weeks.

Serve on salad or steamed vegetables, or use as a dip.

Cost per serving (2 T.): 25¢

NUTRITIONAL ANALYSIS PER SERVING	
Calories: 116	
Fat: 12 grams	
Cholesterol: 3 mg	
Carbohydrates: 1 gram	
Fiber: 1 gram	
Protein: 2 grams	
Sodium: 80 mg	

Kitchen Tip

WORCESTERSHIRE SAUCE got its name from where it was first made: Worcester, England. It is a blend of soy sauce, garlic, onions, molasses, vinegar, anchovies, and lime. It is used in sauces and gravies as well as for a condiment.

Ginger Salad Dressing

Makes 1¾ cups (14 servings)
Preparation Time: 15 minutes

- ½ cup onion chunks
- ½ cup oil
- ⅓ cup vinegar (any type)
- 2 T. water
- 2 T. fresh ginger chunks
- 2 T. celery chunks
- 2 T. ketchup
- 4 tsp. low-sodium soy sauce
- 2 tsp. sugar
- 2 tsp. lemon juice
- 1 clove garlic
- ½ tsp. salt
- ¼ tsp. black pepper

Place all of the ingredients in a blender, cover, and blend for 30 seconds or until smooth. Refrigerate in a tightly covered container.

Serve over salad or steamed vegetables, over stir-fry, over grilled chicken, or even over pasta.

Cost per serving (2 T.): 11¢

NUTRITIONAL ANALYSIS PER SERVING

Calories: 80

Fat: 8 grams

Cholesterol: 0 mg

Carbohydrates: 3 grams

Fiber: 0 grams

Protein: 0 grams

Sodium: 94 mg

 Kitchen Tip

There are three main TYPES OF GARLIC available at most grocery stores. The white-skinned garlic bulbs (American) have the strongest flavor. The purplish colored skinned bulbs (Mexican or Italian) have a milder flavor, and elephant garlic (which is not even a member of the garlic family, but rather of the leek family) has a very mild flavor. Use the one you prefer!

Honey Mustard Dressing

Makes 1⅛ cups (10 servings)
Preparation Time: 10 minutes

- 2 T. honey
- 1 T. prepared mustard
- ⅓ cup vegetable oil
- ½ cup low-fat mayonnaise
- 1 T. cider vinegar
- ½ tsp. minced onions
- 1½ tsp. chopped fresh parsley
- ⅛ tsp. Worcestershire sauce
- pinch of salt

NUTRITIONAL ANALYSIS PER SERVING
Calories: 92
Fat: 8 grams
Cholesterol: 5 mg
Carbohydrates: 5 grams
Fiber: 0 grams
Protein: 0 grams
Sodium: 115 mg

Place all of the ingredients in a small mixing bowl, and whisk together for 30 seconds or until smooth. Refrigerate in a tightly covered container.

Serve over salad or steamed vegetables, use as a dip, or use as a marinade for grilled chicken.

Cost per serving (2 T.): 10¢

Kitchen Tip

PARSLEY, sometimes called Italian parsley or flat leaf parsley, is sold in bunches in the produce section. It should not be confused with Chinese parsley, which is what Americans call cilantro. Parsley has a slightly peppery taste. When buying parsley, choose a bunch that shows no signs of wilting. Rinse it thoroughly, pat dry with a paper towel, and store in the refrigerator in a plastic bag. It will last a week or so. Dried parsley has a poor flavor and does not make a good substitute for fresh.

Mock Clotted Cream

Makes 1½ cups (12 servings)
Preparation Time: 5 minutes

- ½ cup heavy cream
- 2 T. powdered sugar
- ½ cup sour cream

In a bowl, beat cream until soft peaks form (be careful not to beat too long or you will end up with butter). Add sugar and beat only long enough to mix it in well. Fold in the sour cream and mix well.

Store in an airtight container in the refrigerator and it should last 1 to 2 weeks.

Serve on warm scones with jam.

Cost per serving (0.5 ounce): 11¢

NUTRITIONAL ANALYSIS PER SERVING
Calories: 47
Fat: 4 grams
Cholesterol: 16 mg
Carbohydrates: 2 grams
Fiber: 0 grams
Protein: 0 grams
Sodium: 7 mg

Kitchen Tip

To SOFTEN CREAM CHEESE, leave at room temperature for an hour (or longer if the kitchen is cool).

Honey Butter

Makes ½ cup (12 servings)
Preparation Time: 5 minutes

- ¼ cup butter
- ¼ cup honey
- 1 tsp. vanilla extract

Soften the butter. Place all of the ingredients in a bowl or mixer, and whip or blend until smooth and creamy.

Store in an airtight container in the refrigerator. Will last for several weeks.

Serve on warm breads, rolls, or muffins.

Cost per serving (2 tsp.): 8¢

NUTRITIONAL ANALYSIS PER SERVING

Calories: 51

Fat: 4 grams

Cholesterol: 10 mg

Carbohydrates: 6 grams

Fiber: 0 grams

Protein: 0 grams

Sodium: 39 mg

 *Kitchen Tip*

STORING HONEY in a dry place will prevent some crystallization. Honey absorbs moisture, which can lead to crystallizing. If your honey or syrup has already crystallized, place the jar in a pan of hot water until the crystals melt, stirring as needed.

Raspberry Butter

Makes ½ cup (12 servings)
Preparation Time: 5 minutes

- ¼ cup butter
- ⅓ cup seedless raspberry jam

Soften the butter. Place butter and jam in a mixing bowl, and mix until smooth and creamy.

Store in an airtight container in the refrigerator. Will last for several weeks.

Serve on warm breads, rolls, or muffins.

Cost per serving (2 tsp.): 7¢

NUTRITIONAL ANALYSIS PER SERVING
Calories: 54
Fat: 4 grams
Cholesterol: 10 mg
Carbohydrates: 6 grams
Fiber: 0 grams
Protein: 0 grams
Sodium: 40 mg

Kitchen Tip

After cleaning up your kitchen with a sponge, SANITIZE THE SPONGE by adding it to your dishwasher along with the dishes. Lay it on the top rack or place it in the silverware container. The extremely hot water and chlorine in the dish detergent will kill the bacteria that lurk in kitchen sponges.

Loco Chicken Marinade

Makes 1⅓ cups (4 servings)
Preparation Time: 10 minutes

- 2 T. lemon juice
- ¼ cup orange juice
- 2 T. wine vinegar
- 2 T. Worcestershire sauce
- 1 tsp. chili powder
- ½ cup ketchup
- 4 cloves garlic, pressed
- 1 tsp. onion powder
- 1 tsp. hot sauce (see page 204)
- 2 T. oil

NUTRITIONAL ANALYSIS PER SERVING	
Calories: 118	
Fat: 7 grams	
Cholesterol: 0 mg	
Carbohydrates: 15 grams	
Fiber: 1 gram	
Protein: 1 gram	
Sodium: 447 mg	

Combine all of the ingredients in a small mixing bowl.

Suggested use: Pour ⅓ cup of marinade over 2 pounds of chicken pieces or strips; toss so that the chicken is evenly covered with sauce. Cover and marinate in the refrigerator for 4 to 24 hours (the longer the marinating the better the flavor). Bake, grill, or stir-fry the chicken.

Cost per serving (⅓ cup): 34¢

Kitchen Tip

Add a few thin strips of CITRUS ZEST—lemon, lime, or orange peel—to sauces to enhance the flavor.

Sweet and Sour Sauce

Makes 1⅓ cups (4 servings)
Preparation Time: 10 minutes

- 6-oz. can pineapple chunks (reserve liquid)
- ¼ cup brown sugar
- ⅓ cup vinegar (any type)
- 1 T. low-sodium soy sauce
- 2 T. cornstarch

Drain the juice from the can of pineapple into a small saucepan. Combine the pineapple juice, brown sugar, vinegar, soy sauce, and cornstarch in the saucepan. Heat over medium heat, stirring constantly. It will thicken as it boils. Add the pineapple chunks, and stir 1 to 2 minutes to heat the fruit.

Suggested uses: Toss with basic freezer meatballs (see page 99), or serve over any other meat, tofu, or TVP chunks. Also good as a salad dressing or over chow mein noodles.

Cost per serving (⅓ cup): 13¢

NUTRITIONAL ANALYSIS PER SERVING
Calories: 98
Fat: 0 grams
Cholesterol: 0 mg
Carbohydrates: 25 grams
Fiber: 1 gram
Protein: 1 gram
Sodium: 212 mg

Kitchen Tip

You can EASILY MAKE A SAUCE after cooking any type of chicken, meat, or fish in a skillet. When you are done cooking the meat, remove the meat and add ¼ cup of wine or broth to the pan drippings. Cook for 2 to 3 minutes, and pour over the meat.

Lemon Garlic Salad Dressing

Makes ½ cup (4 servings)
Preparation Time: 10 minutes
Recipe donated by Joan Stivers

- 2 T. lemon juice
- 1 clove garlic
- ½ tsp. dried oregano
- ½ tsp. prepared mustard (Dijon tastes best)
- ¼ cup olive oil
- 2 T. water

Place all ingredients in a blender. Cover and blend on high for 1 to 2 minutes or until the dressing is creamy and smooth.

Serve immediately over salad or steamed vegetables.

Note: This can be stored in the refrigerator, but will need to be blended again before serving, as the ingredients separate.

Cost per serving (2 T.): 19¢

NUTRITIONAL ANALYSIS PER SERVING
Calories: 124
Fat: 13 grams
Cholesterol: 0 mg
Carbohydrates: 1 gram
Fiber: 0 grams
Protein: 0 grams
Sodium: 8 mg

Kitchen Tip

Try different liquids in sauce recipes IN PLACE OF WATER that is called for to add a richer flavor. Use diluted fruit juice, soup, stock, tea, or wine.

Teriyaki Sauce

Makes 2⅛ cups (4 servings)
Preparation Time: 10 minutes

- ½ cup water, divided
- 2 T. cornstarch
- ¾ cup honey
- ½ cup low-sodium soy sauce
- ¼ cup wine vinegar
- ½ tsp. onion powder
- ½ tsp. ginger powder

NUTRITIONAL ANALYSIS PER SERVING
Calories: 101
Fat: 0 grams
Cholesterol: 0 mg
Carbohydrates: 27 grams
Fiber: 0 grams
Protein: 1 gram
Sodium: 432 mg

In a small bowl, mix ¼ cup of the water with the cornstarch.

In a shallow saucepan over medium heat, combine the honey, the rest of the water, soy sauce, vinegar, and onion and ginger powders. Whisk together. Add the cornstarch mixture. While constantly stirring, heat the mixture to a boil. Boil, while stirring, for 1 to 3 minutes. It will thicken as it boils.

Store in a covered container in the refrigerator. Will keep for several months.

Use as a marinade or basting sauce for chicken or meat, or brush it on vegetables or meat.

Cost per serving (¼ cup): 9¢

Kitchen Tip

If a recipe calls for wine, or you wish to use a bit of wine in a sauce to enhance the flavor, AVOID COOKING WINES—they are not true wines. Cooking wines have salt, flavoring, and preservatives added to them, and can ruin a recipe.

Meat Rub

Makes ½ cup (8 servings)
Preparation Time: 10 minutes

- ¼ cup fresh parsley leaves
- 1 T. Italian seasoning (see page 209)
- 1 T. lemon juice
- 2 cloves garlic
- 1 tsp. pepper
- 1 T. cumin seeds or 2 tsp. ground cumin
- 1 T. oil
- 1 tsp. salt

Combine all of the ingredients in a food processor or blender that can handle small amounts, or use a pestle and mortar. Blend to form a paste.

To use, spread 1 tablespoon (or more to taste) of mix over a 2-pound roast (either beef or chicken) before baking.

Cost per serving (1 T.): 9¢

NUTRITIONAL ANALYSIS PER SERVING
Calories: 24
Fat: 2 grams
Cholesterol: 0 mg
Carbohydrates: 2 grams
Fiber: 1 gram
Protein: 1 gram
Sodium: 246 mg

Kitchen Tip

Make GRAVY from the meat drippings in the pan after the meat has been roasted. Remove any fat from the pan, then add 1 to 2 cups of stock; let it simmer for 5 to 10 minutes to loosen the drippings. Continue cooking to reduce the amount of liquid. If you like thicker gravy, add 1 to 2 tablespoons of flour that have been mixed with 2 tablespoons of liquid first, or add 1 to 2 tablespoons of instant mashed potatoes.

Memphis BBQ Sauce

Makes 5 cups (20 servings)
Preparation Time: 10 minutes

- 1 cup Worcestershire sauce
- 2½ cups ketchup
- 1 cup brown sugar
- ½ cup prepared mustard
- 1 T. salt
- 1 T. pepper

Combine all of the ingredients in a bowl and mix well.

Store any unused portion covered in the refrigerator.

Cost per serving (¼ cup): 12¢

NUTRITIONAL ANALYSIS
PER SERVING

Calories: 87

Fat: 0 grams

Cholesterol: 0 mg

Carbohydrates: 22 grams

Fiber: 0 grams

Protein: 1 gram

Sodium: 892 mg

Kitchen Tip

To soften HARDENED BROWN SUGAR, place a slice of bread in the container with the sugar and seal.

Lemon Pepper Marinade

Makes ⅔ cup (2 servings)
Preparation Time: 10 minutes

- 2 T. olive oil
- ¼ cup minced onion
- 1 clove garlic, pressed
- ½ tsp. pepper
- 2 T. Italian seasoning (see page 209)
- ¼ cup lemon juice
- 1 tsp. sugar

Combine all of the ingredients in a bowl. Store in an airtight container if you won't be using it right away.

To use: Pour ⅓ cup of marinade over fish or meat, and let marinate for at least 30 minutes. Use some to baste the meat or fish while it is cooking.

Cost per serving (⅓ cup): 55¢

NUTRITIONAL ANALYSIS PER SERVING

Calories: 39

Fat: 4 grams

Cholesterol: 0 mg

Carbohydrates: 3 grams

Fiber: 1 gram

Protein: 0 grams

Sodium: 35 mg

Kitchen Tip

MARINADES serve two purposes. First, to add flavor to the meat. Second, to tenderize the meat. In order for a marinade to tenderize, it must have an acidic component in it. The longer the meat sits in the acidic solution, the more tender it will become. Since acid reacts with aluminum, don't marinate in an aluminum pan.

Hot Sauce

Makes 4 cups (32 servings)
Preparation Time: 5 minutes
Cooking Time: 5 minutes

- 6-oz. can tomato paste
- 3 cups water
- 2 tsp. cayenne pepper
- 1 T. chili powder
- 2 tsp. salt
- 2 tsp. cornstarch
- 2 tsp. distilled white vinegar
- 2 tsp. onion powder

NUTRITIONAL ANALYSIS PER SERVING
Calories: 7
Fat: 0 grams
Cholesterol: 0 mg
Carbohydrates: 2 grams
Fiber: 0 grams
Protein: 0 grams
Sodium: 140 mg

In a medium saucepan, combine all of the ingredients. Mix well. Heat the sauce to boiling over medium heat while constantly stirring. Continue to boil and stir for 2 to 3 minutes or until it thickens.

Remove from heat. Let cool. If you like a smooth texture, puree the sauce in a blender. Pour into a jar with an airtight lid, and store in the refrigerator for up to 3 months.

Option: If you like your hot sauce hotter, increase the cayenne pepper to suit your taste. Or, you can add a diced jalapeño or habanero pepper to the sauce before cooking.

Cost per serving (2 T.): 2¢

Kitchen Tip

Vinegar is produced by bacteria in a fermenting liquid (apple juice, wine, grain, beer, etc.). Different types of vinegar give foods different flavors. But all of them are acidic and corrosive so should not be put in copper, aluminum, zinc, or iron pans. DISTILLED VINEGAR is made from grains and is commonly used in pickling foods due to its milder flavor. CIDER VINEGAR is made from malt or apple juice and is more acidic than distilled vinegars. WINE VINEGAR is made from either red or white wine and has a mild flavor. MALT VINEGAR is made from malted barley (beer). RICE VINEGAR is made from fermented rice. BALSAMIC VINEGAR is made from grape juice and has a sweet and pungent flavor that has made it very popular.

Spaghetti Sauce

Makes 4¾ cups (6 servings)
Preparation Time: 10 minutes
Cooking Time: 35 minutes

- 1 T. oil
- 1 medium onion, diced
- 2 cloves garlic, pressed
- 28-oz. can tomatoes, diced (do not drain)
- 6-oz. can tomato paste
- 2 tsp. red wine vinegar
- 3 T. Italian seasoning (see page 209)
- 1 T. sugar
- 1 tsp. salt
- ½ tsp. pepper

NUTRITIONAL ANALYSIS
PER SERVING

Calories: 89

Fat: 3 grams

Cholesterol: 0 mg

Carbohydrates: 16 grams

Fiber: 3 grams

Protein: 3 grams

Sodium: 682 mg

In a large saucepan, heat the oil over medium heat. Add onion and garlic, and sauté for 2 to 3 minutes or until the garlic is golden brown. Add the remaining ingredients, and stir to mix. Simmer, stirring occasionally, for 30 minutes. If it thickens too much for your taste, add up to ½ cup water.

This can also be used as a pizza sauce.

Cost per serving (¾ cup): 43¢

Kitchen Tip

You can use 1½ lb. FRESH TOMA-TOES, peeled and diced, instead of the 28 ounces of canned tomatoes called for in most recipes.

Pesto Sauce

Makes 1½ cups (6 servings)
Preparation Time: 10 minutes

- 2 cups packed fresh basil leaves
- ½ cup olive oil
- 3 cloves garlic, pressed
- ½ cup pine nuts or walnuts
- ½ tsp. salt
- ½ tsp. pepper
- ½ tsp. lemon juice

Wash the basil leaves and remove and discard the stems.

Put the basil in the blender, and then add all the other ingredients. Blend until the sauce is creamy and well blended. Cover and store any unused portion in the refrigerator.

To use: Toss over warm pasta, spread on toasted sourdough bread, use instead of a tomato-based sauce on pizza, or spread over chicken while baking.

Cost per serving (¼ cup): 32¢

NUTRITIONAL ANALYSIS PER SERVING	
Calories: 191	
Fat: 20 grams	
Cholesterol: 0 mg	
Carbohydrates: 3 grams	
Fiber: 0 grams	
Protein: 2 grams	
Sodium: 180 mg	

Kitchen Tip

Fresh BASIL LEAVES have a strong flavor. Do not substitute dried basil for fresh in a pesto recipe. There are many varieties of basil, including LEMON BASIL, that would add a nice flavor to a pesto dish. Basil can be grown indoors all year or outdoors in the summer. Once picked, the leaves can be stored for one week in the refrigerator.

Sweetened Condensed Milk

Makes 2 cups (16 servings)
Preparation Time: 15 minutes

- ⅔ cups granulated sugar
- ⅓ cup water
- 3 T. margarine
- 1 cup powdered sugar

Combine the first three ingredients in a saucepan. Bring to a boil and simmer until the sugar is dissolved. Remove from the heat and pour into a blender. Add the powdered sugar and blend until smooth. Cover and store in the refrigerator for 1 to 2 weeks.

Cost per serving (2 T.): 9¢

NUTRITIONAL ANALYSIS PER SERVING	
Calories: 230	
Fat: 4 grams	
Cholesterol: 5 mg	
Carbohydrates: 45 grams	
Fiber: 0 grams	
Protein: 8 grams	
Sodium: 140 mg	

Kitchen Tip

To guard yourself against burns while BLENDING HOT LIQUIDS, let the liquid cool a bit before blending (either with a tabletop blender or a hand-held one). If the contents of a blender are very hot, they will expand while covered and burst the lid off of the blender, splashing hot liquid on you and the kitchen walls.

CHAPTER 12

Mixes

Italian Seasoning

Makes 1 ⅛ cups
Preparation Time: 5 minutes

- ¼ cup dried basil
- 2 T. dried sage
- ¼ cup dried thyme
- ¼ cup dried rosemary
- ¼ cup dried oregano

Put all of the ingredients in a blender, cover, and blend until powdery (don't over blend). Use the "pulse" feature if your blender has one. This should take 5 seconds or less.

Store in an airtight container. This will keep for several months.

Cost per serving (1 tsp.): 4¢

NUTRITIONAL ANALYSIS PER SERVING
Calories: 4
Fat: 0 grams
Cholesterol: 0 mg
Carbohydrates: 1 gram
Fiber: 0 grams
Protein: 0 grams
Sodium: 1 mg

Kitchen Tip

SAGE is a strong herb with a musty flavor. It is used in both cooking and medicine. It is excellent with poultry, pasta, sausage, beans, cheese, stuffing, and most vegetables. It can be made into a tea as well. It can be used fresh or dried. The longer it is stored, the less flavor it will have.

Homemade Bread Crumbs

Makes 1 cup
Preparation Time: 5 minutes
This is a great way to use ends of loaves or dried-out bread.

- 2 slices bread

Tear bread into medium-sized pieces and place in blender. Cover and blend on low speed until all the bread is in crumbs.

These can be stored in the freezer for up to six months.

To make SEASONED BREAD CRUMBS add the following ingredients to the blender:

- ½ tsp. salt
- ½ tsp. dried parsley
- ¼ tsp. garlic powder
- ¼ tsp. onion powder
- ¼ tsp. Italian seasoning (see previous page)

Note: There is a difference between dry and fresh bread crumbs. Dry bread crumbs are made from dried bread. They are more absorbent than fresh bread crumbs. Use fresh (not dried) bread for all recipes in *Healthy Meals for Less* that call for bread crumbs.

Cost per serving (2 T.): 2¢

NUTRITIONAL ANALYSIS PER SERVING
Calories: 16
Fat: 0 grams
Cholesterol: 0 mg
Carbohydrates: 3 grams
Fiber: 0 grams
Protein: 1 gram
Sodium: 34 mg

Kitchen Tip

Save the ends of bread loaves in the freezer. When you need FRESH BREAD CRUMBS, pull the bread out, microwave for a few seconds to thaw, and then proceed with the recipe above.

Shake-On Chicken Coating

Makes 1 mix
Preparation Time: 5 minutes

- 1 cup homemade bread crumbs (see previous recipe)
- 1 tsp. dried parsley
- ¼ tsp. paprika
- ¼ tsp. sugar

Place all of the ingredients in a mixing bowl and mix well.

Suggested use: Place the mix in a plastic bag that can be sealed. Coat ½ pound of chicken pieces with 1 tablespoon of oil. Place one piece of chicken at a time in the bag, seal it, and shake the coating over the chicken until evenly coated. Place the chicken on an ungreased baking sheet. Bake at 350° for 30 to 35 minutes or until done.

Cost per batch (1 cup): 21¢

NUTRITIONAL ANALYSIS PER SERVING
Calories: 146
Fat: 2 grams
Cholesterol: 2 mg
Carbohydrates: 25 grams
Fiber: 1 gram
Protein: 4 grams
Sodium: 274 mg

 *Kitchen Tip*

STORE HERBS AND SPICES in an airtight container in a cool and dry location. Dried herbs lose their flavor after about a year.

Salt-Free Seasoning

Makes 1 cup
Preparation Time: 10 minutes

- ½ cup dried onion flakes
- 2 T. garlic powder
- 1 T. black pepper
- 1 T. dried parsley
- 2 T. Italian seasoning (see page 209)
- 1 tsp. cumin
- 1 tsp. coriander
- ½ tsp. celery seed
- ½ tsp. cayenne pepper
- ¼ tsp. vitamin C powder (ascorbic acid)
- ½ tsp. sugar

Place all of the ingredients in a blender or food processor, and blend until well mixed. Store in an airtight container for up to six months (save an empty spice bottle to use for this mix).

Cost per serving (½ tsp.): 2¢

NUTRITIONAL ANALYSIS PER SERVING	
Calories: 2	
Fat: 0 grams	
Cholesterol: 0 mg	
Carbohydrates: 1 gram	
Fiber: 0 grams	
Protein: 0 grams	
Sodium: 0 mg	

Kitchen Tip

VITAMIN C POWDER (ascorbic acid) is sold in bulk at health food stores. It is expensive but lasts for several years if kept out of direct light. It can be added to juices for the daily requirement of vitamin C, mixed with salt to make lemon salt, which is used for seasoning, or used to roll candies in for sour candies (see gummie squares recipe on page 239).

Fajita Seasoning Mix

Makes 5 mixes
Preparation Time: 10 minutes

- 4 T. chili powder
- 2 T. cumin powder
- 2 tsp. ground oregano
- 2 tsp. garlic salt

Put all of the ingredients in a blender, cover, and blend 5 seconds or less until powdery (don't over blend). Use the "pulse" feature if your blender has one.

Store in an airtight container for up to 6 months.

Two to three tablespoons of this mix equals one purchased packet of fajita seasoning mix.

Cost per mix (5 mixes): 40¢
Cost per serving (2 T.): 8¢

NUTRITIONAL ANALYSIS PER SERVING
Calories: 40
Fat: 2 grams
Cholesterol: 0 mg
Carbohydrates: 7 grams
Fiber: 3 grams
Protein: 2 grams
Sodium: 371 mg

Kitchen Tip

PROOFING YEAST isn't necessary anymore. Proofing was the action of dissolving yeast in water to let it bubble. The dry yeast sold today can be mixed directly into the flour.

Spaghetti Sauce Mix

Makes 4 mixes
Preparation Time: 5 minutes

- ¼ cup Italian seasoning (see page 209)
- 1 T. celery salt
- 1 T. garlic powder
- 1½ tsp. pepper
- 1 T. onion powder
- 1 tsp. sugar

Put all of the ingredients in a blender, cover, and blend 5 seconds or less until powdery (don't over-blend). Use the "pulse" feature if your blender has one.

Store in an airtight container for up to 6 months.

To use: Add 2 tablespoons to 28 ounces of tomato sauce, 6 ounces tomato paste, and any meat or vegetables you like in your sauce. Simmer for 10 minutes over medium heat; serve over pasta.

Cost per mix (2 T.): 12¢
Cost per serving (½ T.): 3¢

NUTRITIONAL ANALYSIS PER SERVING
Calories: 3
Fat: 0 grams
Cholesterol: 0 mg
Carbohydrates: 1 gram
Fiber: 0 grams
Protein: 0 grams
Sodium: 114 mg

Kitchen Tip

AVOID ALUMINUM PANS while cooking tomato-based dishes. The acid in the tomatoes reacts with the aluminum and can change the flavor of the sauce.

Mexican Seasoning Mix

Makes 5 mixes
Preparation Time: 10 minutes
This can be used for either taco or chili seasoning.

- ¼ cup flour
- 2 T. chili powder
- ¼ cup onion powder
- 2 tsp. garlic powder
- 4 tsp. salt
- 4 tsp. paprika
- ½ tsp. cayenne pepper
- 2 tsp. sugar
- 2 tsp. cumin
- 2 tsp. oregano

NUTRITIONAL ANALYSIS PER SERVING
Calories: 19
Fat: 0 grams
Cholesterol: 0 mg
Carbohydrates: 4 grams
Fiber: 1 gram
Protein: 1 gram
Sodium: 128 mg

Put all of the ingredients in a blender, cover, and blend 5 seconds or less until powdery (don't over blend). Use the "pulse" feature if your blender has one. Add more cayenne pepper if you prefer it hotter.

Store in an airtight container for up to 6 months.

Three tablespoons of this mix equals one purchased packet of taco or chili seasoning mix.

Cost per mix (3 T.): 28¢
Cost per serving (2½ tsp.): 9¢

Kitchen Tip

GIFTS FROM YOUR KITCHEN cost considerably less than store-bought gifts and show a personal touch. Be creative with what you make: baked fruit breads wrapped in colorful cellophane and tied with a ribbon; an assortment of candies or cookies in a colorful wrapping; layered cookie mixes in a jar decorated with a cloth and ribbon on the lid; drink mixes or hot fudge sauce (see recipes in this book) in a variety of attractive jars found at hobby stores.

Dough Enhancer

Makes 5⅓ cups
Preparation Time: 5 minutes
Recipe reprinted by permission from Dinner's in the Freezer
by Jill Bond (Hibbard Publishing)

- 4 cups powdered milk
- ¾ cup lecithin granules
- 3 heaping T. vitamin C powder (ascorbic acid)
- 2 T. powdered ginger
- 3 T. cornstarch

Dough enhancer helps dough rise better and gives it a fluffier texture. It is very helpful with whole wheat bread recipes that need an extra lift. Store-bought dough enhancer costs a tremendous amount more than homemade.

Put all of the ingredients in a blender, and blend on medium for 30 seconds or until well blended. Store in an airtight container for up to 6 months.

Add 1 tablespoon of dough enhancer per loaf of bread. Add to the dough along with the flour.

Cost per serving (1 T.): 4¢

NUTRITIONAL ANALYSIS PER SERVING
Calories: 50
Fat: 4 grams
Cholesterol: 6 mg
Carbohydrates: 3 grams
Fiber: 0 grams
Protein: 2 grams
Sodium: 23 mg

Kitchen Tip

LECITHIN is a fatty substance found in soybeans and egg yolks. Even though it is a fat, it acts as an emulsifier for other fats. It is added to foods such as bread dough (above) to aid in the mixing of the dough, making a better texture. Lecithin is also an element needed by human cells for proper functioning and is taken as a supplement.

Swiss Mocha Mix

Makes 17 mixes
Preparation Time: 5 minutes

- ½ cup instant coffee powder
- ½ cup sugar
- 1 cup powdered milk
- 2 T. cocoa powder (unsweetened)

Put all of the ingredients in a blender, cover, and blend until powdery. This should take 15 seconds or less.

Store in an airtight container for up to six months.

To use: Add 2 tablespoons of mix to ⅔ cup hot water, and stir.

Cost per serving (2 T.): 9¢

NUTRITIONAL ANALYSIS PER SERVING
Calories: 41
Fat: 0 grams
Cholesterol: 1 mg
Carbohydrates: 9 grams
Fiber: 0 grams
Protein: 2 grams
Sodium: 24 mg

Kitchen Tip

If a recipe calls for UNSWEET-ENED CHOCOLATE SQUARES and all you have is cocoa powder, use the following conversion chart: 1 ounce chocolate square = 3 tablespoons cocoa powder plus 1 tablespoon butter.

Hot Cocoa Mix

Makes 24 mixes
Preparation Time: 5 minutes

- 1 cup sugar
- 2 cups powdered milk
- ¾ cup cocoa powder (unsweetened)

Put all of the ingredients in a blender, cover, and blend until powdery. This should take 15 seconds or less.

Store in an airtight container for up to six months.

To use: Add 2 to 3 tablespoons of mix to ⅔ cup hot water, and stir.

Note: If giving this mix as a gift, layer the mix with miniature marshmallows in a clear jar to give it a "sand art" appearance. Attach an attractive instruction card with a ribbon.

Cost per serving (2½ T.): 16¢

NUTRITIONAL ANALYSIS PER SERVING

Calories: 117

Fat: 1 gram

Cholesterol: 2 mg

Carbohydrates: 26 grams

Fiber: 2 grams

Protein: 5 grams

Sodium: 63 mg

 Kitchen Tip

For a delicious COLD DRINK, add to a cup of chilled hot cocoa: a dash of cinnamon, a dash of vanilla, and 1 cup of nondairy whipped topping (e.g., Cool Whip). Blend gently as you mix together. Garnish with a sprinkle of cinnamon.

Cappuccino Mix

Makes 18 mixes
Preparation Time: 5 minutes

- ¾ cup sugar
- 1 cup powdered milk
- ½ cup instant coffee powder
- 1 tsp. cinnamon
- 1 tsp. dried orange peel

Put all of the ingredients in a blender, cover, and blend until powdery. This should take 15 seconds or less.

Store in an airtight container for up to six months.

To use: Add 2 tablespoons of mix to ⅔ cup hot water, and stir.

Cost per serving (2 T.): 7¢

NUTRITIONAL ANALYSIS PER SERVING	
Calories: 42	
Fat: 0 grams	
Cholesterol: 1 mg	
Carbohydrates: 9 grams	
Fiber: 0 grams	
Protein: 1 gram	
Sodium: 19 mg	

Kitchen Tip

For CAPPUCCINO COCOA, add 1 T. hot cocoa mix to a prepared mug of this mix.

Café Bavarian Mint Mix

Makes 10 mixes
Preparation Time: 5 minutes

- 2 hard peppermint candy canes
- ¼ cup powdered creamer
- ⅓ cup sugar
- ¼ cup instant coffee powder
- 2 T. cocoa powder

Break the candy canes into 1-inch pieces. Put all of the ingredients in a blender, cover, and blend until powdery.

Store in an airtight container for up to six months.

To use: Add 2 tablespoons of mix to ⅔ cup hot water, and stir.

Note: For gift giving, put in a decorative jar. Attach an attractive instruction card with a ribbon.

Cost per serving (2 T.): 9¢

**NUTRITIONAL ANALYSIS
PER SERVING**

Calories: 61

Fat: 1 gram

Cholesterol: 0 mg

Carbohydrates: 15 grams

Fiber: 0 grams

Protein: 0 grams

Sodium: 3 mg

 Kitchen Tip

STIR YOUR COFFEE with a peppermint stick to add a nice flavor and elegant look.

Onion Soup Mix

Makes 10 mixes
Preparation Time: 5 minutes

- 2¼ cups dried minced onion
- 1 cup broth powder (see page 226)
- ¼ cup onion powder
- ¾ tsp. celery seed
- ¾ tsp. sugar

Combine all of the ingredients in a bowl using a large spoon. Store in an airtight container for up to 6 months.

To use: Stir ⅓ cup of the mix into 2 cups hot water in a medium saucepan. Bring to a boil over medium heat, and boil for 1 minute. Reduce heat and simmer for 10 minutes.

In recipes where a 1.25-ounce envelope of purchased onion soup mix is required, use ⅓ cup of this mix.

Cost per mix (⅓ cup): 43¢
Cost per serving (4 tsp.): 11¢

**NUTRITIONAL ANALYSIS
PER SERVING**

Calories: 15

Fat: 0 grams

Cholesterol: 0 mg

Carbohydrates: 4 grams

Fiber: 0 grams

Protein: 1 gram

Sodium: 9 mg

Kitchen Tip

To make ONION DIP, mix ⅓ cup of onion soup mix with 2 cups of sour cream. The flavor is enhanced if it sits overnight in the refrigerator.

Chicken-Flavored Rice Mix

Makes 3 mixes
Preparation Time: 5 minutes

- 4 cups white rice (not instant)
- ¼ cup broth powder (see page 226)
- 1 T. Italian seasoning mix (see page 209)
- ¼ tsp. pepper

Combine all of the ingredients in a bowl using a large spoon. Store in an airtight container for up to 6 months.

To use: Shake the mix to distribute the herbs. Mix 1⅓ cup of the mix with 2 cups hot water in a medium saucepan. Add 1 tablespoon butter. Bring to a boil over medium heat and boil for 1 minute. Reduce heat and simmer for 15 minutes.

Cost per mix (1⅓ cup): 49¢
Cost per serving (½ cup prepared): 12¢

NUTRITIONAL ANALYSIS PER SERVING
Calories: 232
Fat: 0 grams
Cholesterol: 0 mg
Carbohydrates: 50 grams
Fiber: 1 gram
Protein: 5 grams
Sodium: 9 mg

Kitchen Tip

The different TYPES OF RICE can be confusing: There is long-grain, medium-grain, and short-grain rice, each referring to its size. Within each category there is brown rice and white rice. Brown rice means that the entire kernel is present except the outer inedible husk. White rice has had the germ and bran removed in addition to the husk. Some special types that deserve mention are basmati (long-grain white rice from Asia with a slight perfume taste and smell) and pearl (short-grain white rice from China and easy to pick up with chopsticks). Instant rice has been partially cooked, then dehydrated.

Ranch Salad Dressing Mix

Makes 4 mixes
Preparation Time: 5 minutes

- 16 saltine crackers
- ½ cup dried parsley
- 2 T. onion powder
- 2 T. garlic powder
- 1 tsp. pepper
- 2 tsp. salt

Combine all of the ingredients in a blender, cover, and blend until powdery.

To use: Combine ¼ cup of mix with ¾ cup buttermilk and 1 cup mayonnaise. Blend well, and let sit for a few minutes before serving.

This mix can also be used to coat chicken prior to cooking, or in any other recipe where ranch dressing mix is called for.

Cost per mix (¼ cup): 49¢
Cost per serving of mix (1 T.): 12¢

NUTRITIONAL ANALYSIS PER SERVING
Calories: 10
Fat: 0 grams
Cholesterol: 0 mg
Carbohydrates: 2 grams
Fiber: 0 grams
Protein: 0 grams
Sodium: 126 mg

Kitchen Tip

A good SUBSTITUTE FOR BUTTERMILK is plain yogurt. It has the same tartness and acidity that buttermilk provides.

Liquid Flavored Creamer

Serves 36
Preparation Time: 5 minutes

- 12-oz. can evaporated milk
- 2 tsp. chocolate syrup (see page 248)
- ½ tsp. vanilla

Place all of the ingredients in a blender, cover, and blend until well mixed. Store in airtight jar in the refrigerator for up to a week.

To use: Add 2 teaspoons creamer to a cup of coffee.

Variations: For vanilla-flavored creamer, omit the chocolate and increase the vanilla to 2 teaspoons; for amaretto flavoring, omit the vanilla and chocolate and add 2 teaspoons almond extract.

Cost per serving (2 tsp.): 3¢

NUTRITIONAL ANALYSIS PER SERVING
Calories: 14
Fat: 1 gram
Cholesterol: 3 mg
Carbohydrates: 1 gram
Fiber: 0 grams
Protein: 1 gram
Sodium: 10 mg

 Kitchen Tip

To make FLAVORED COFFEES more affordable, add flavoring to the cream instead of buying flavored coffee.

Powdered Flavored Creamer

Serves 36
Preparation Time: 5 minutes

Base Creamer:

- ¾ cup powdered nondairy coffee creamer
- ¾ cup powdered sugar

Place both ingredients in a blender, cover, and blend until well mixed.

To make flavored creamers, add one of the following to the base creamer, and blend again.

Bavarian Mint Coffee Creamer

- ½ cup cocoa powder, unsweetened
- ½ tsp. peppermint extract

Amaretto Coffee Creamer

- 1 tsp. cinnamon
- 1 tsp. almond extract

Chocolate Raspberry Coffee Creamer

- ½ cup cocoa powder, unsweetened
- ½ tsp. raspberry flavoring

Store in an airtight container in the refrigerator for up to two months.

To use: Add 2 teaspoons to a cup of coffee.

Cost per serving (2 tsp.): 3¢

NUTRITIONAL ANALYSIS PER SERVING
Calories: 20
Fat: 1 gram
Cholesterol: 0 mg
Carbohydrates: 4 grams
Fiber: 0 grams
Protein: 0 grams
Sodium: 4 mg

Kitchen Tip

PEPPERMINT AND SPEARMINT should not be used interchangeably. Each has a unique flavor.

Broth Powder

Makes 1⅔ cups
Preparation Time: 10 minutes
This recipe has a fraction of the sodium that commercial broth powders or bouillon does. DO NOT USE PURCHASED BROTH POWDER WHERE BROTH POWDER IS CALLED FOR WITHOUT ADJUSTING THE SALT. Use the conversion notes below.

- 1 cup nutritional yeast flakes (see tip below)
- 3 T. onion powder
- 1 T. garlic powder
- 1 T. salt
- 1 tsp. celery seed
- 2 T. Italian seasoning (see page 209)
- 2 T. dried parsley
- ½ tsp. pepper
- 1 tsp. marjoram
- 1 tsp. tarragon
- 1 tsp. paprika

NUTRITIONAL ANALYSIS PER SERVING	
Calories: 20	
Fat: 0 grams	
Cholesterol: 0 mg	
Carbohydrates: 3 grams	
Fiber: 2 grams	
Protein: 2 grams	
Sodium: 251 mg	

Place all of the ingredients in a blender, cover, and blend for 3 to 4 seconds, or until well mixed. Store in an airtight jar for up to 6 months.

To use: Add 1 tablespoon to a cup of hot water for a cup of soup or stock.

Conversion Note: Two teaspoons of this recipe plus ½ teaspoon of salt is the equivalent of 1 bouillon cube.

To use commercial broth powder in place of homemade broth powder called for in a recipe, reduce the salt in the recipe by ½ teaspoon for every 2 teaspoons of commercial broth powder used.

Cost per serving (1 T.): 13¢

 *Kitchen Tip*

NUTRITIONAL YEAST, also known as brewer's yeast, is a nutritional product eaten for its high content of the B vitamins, amino acids, and protein. It is not to be confused with or used in the same way as baking yeast. Nutritional yeast is grown from the grain hops. It can be sprinkled on foods or mixed in juice to increase its nutritional value. It is sold in health food stores and some traditional grocery stores.

CHAPTER 13

Desserts and Snacks

Almost Nutri-Grain Bars

Makes 15 bars
Preparation Time: 15 minutes
Cooking Time: 40 minutes

- 1 cup rolled oats
- 1 cup whole wheat flour
- ⅔ cup brown sugar
- ½ tsp. baking soda
- ½ tsp. salt
- ¼ cup oil
- 1 egg
- 1 tsp. vanilla
- ¼ cup apple juice
- 10 oz. jam (apricot, blackberry, blueberry, raspberry, strawberry, or apple butter)
- 1 T. water

NUTRITIONAL ANALYSIS PER SERVING	
Calories: 176	
Fat: 5 grams	
Cholesterol: 12 mg	
Carbohydrates: 32 grams	
Fiber: 1 gram	
Protein: 3 grams	
Sodium: 127 mg	

Combine oats, flour, brown sugar, baking soda, and salt in a bowl and mix thoroughly. Add the oil, egg, vanilla, and apple juice, and mix with a spoon or a mixer. Press ⅔ of the mix evenly into a greased 8x12 pan. Mix the jam with the water, and spread evenly over the mix. Crumble the remaining oat mixture over the top, and bake at 325° for 30 to 40 minutes or until golden brown. Before cutting, cool completely.

Cost per serving (1 bar): 15¢

Kitchen Tip

Most cookie dough recipes can be baked as a BAR COOKIE, but not all bar-cookie recipes can be baked as individual cookies. To make bar cookies with a cookie dough recipe, spread dough in a 9x13 pan and bake 20 to 30 minutes or until golden brown.

Chewy Granola Bars

Makes 6 bars
Preparation Time: 10 minutes
Cooking Time: 20 minutes

- 1 cup rolled oats
- ½ cup whole wheat flour
- ½ cup brown sugar, firmly packed
- ¼ tsp. baking soda
- ¼ tsp. baking powder
- ½ tsp. cinnamon
- ¼ tsp. nutmeg
- ½ tsp. salt
- ½ tsp. vanilla
- ¼ cup honey

NUTRITIONAL ANALYSIS PER SERVING	
Calories: 225	
Fat: 2 grams	
Cholesterol: 0 mg	
Carbohydrates: 48 grams	
Fiber: 1 gram	
Protein: 6 grams	
Sodium: 252 mg	

Combine oats, flour, brown sugar, baking soda, baking powder, cinnamon, nutmeg, and salt in a bowl, and mix. Add the vanilla and honey, and mix well. Press the mix evenly into a greased 8x8 pan. Bake at 325° for 18 to 20 minutes or until golden brown. Before cutting, cool completely.

Option: Add 1 cup of any of the following when you add the honey: chopped nuts, dried fruit, chocolate chips, or coconut.

Cost per serving (1 bar): 14¢

 *Kitchen Tip*

To make granola bars or brownies special, add a CHOCOLATE TOPPING: Put 1 to 2 of your favorite candy bars in a bowl, add 1 to 2 tablespoons of milk, and melt in the microwave. (My favorites are Nestlé Crunch, Mr. Goodbar, and Butterfinger.) Mix and spread over the bars or brownies.

To-Die-For Brownies

Makes 36 bars
Preparation Time: 10 minutes
Cooking Time: 40 minutes

- 6 eggs
- 1 cup butter, melted
- ½ cup vegetable oil
- 4 cups sugar
- 1 T. vanilla extract
- 3 cups flour
- 1½ cups cocoa powder
- 2 tsp. salt

NUTRITIONAL ANALYSIS PER SERVING	
Calories: 214	
Fat: 9 grams	
Cholesterol: 44 mg	
Carbohydrates: 32 grams	
Fiber: 2 grams	
Protein: 3 grams	
Sodium: 180 mg	

In a mixing bowl, combine the eggs, butter, oil, sugar, and vanilla. Mix well. Add the rest of the ingredients, and mix until well blended.

Spread the batter evenly in a greased 9x13 pan.

Bake at 350° for 40 minutes or until a toothpick inserted in the center comes out clean. Do not over bake.

Cost per serving (1 brownie): 13¢

Kitchen Tip

To EASILY GREASE PANS, place a small amount of butter or shortening on a paper towel. Rub the shortening evenly over the bottom and sides of the pan. Discard the paper towel when done.

Raspberry Soufflé

Serves 4
Preparation Time: 25 minutes
Cooking Time: 15 minutes

- ½ cup seedless raspberry jam (blackberry and boysenberry also taste good)
- 3 egg whites
- ½ cup sugar

In a small bowl, melt the jam in the microwave. Do not boil it. Set aside.

Place egg whites in a mixing bowl and whip with a mixer until stiff and forming peaks. Add the sugar into the egg white mixture slowly while beating. Remove the beaters, and fold the jam into the egg white mixture with a spatula. Don't overmix, or the air will disappear and the soufflé will fall.

Scoop the mixture into a greased 8x8 pan, and bake at 325° for 15 minutes or until golden brown on top. Serve immediately while hot.

Option: Serve with some more melted jam drizzled over the top for a nice presentation and added flavor.

Cost per serving (¾ cup): 28¢

NUTRITIONAL ANALYSIS PER SERVING

Calories: 206

Fat: 0 grams

Cholesterol: 0 mg

Carbohydrates: 51 grams

Fiber: 0 grams

Protein: 3 grams

Sodium: 58 mg

 *Kitchen Tip*

SOUFFLÉ is a general term to describe a dish that has trapped air inside, achieved with beaten egg whites. The soufflé can have varying ingredients added to it, and can be served hot or cold. Most soufflés are served with a sauce to soften the dry nature of the dish.

Energy Bar

Makes 8 bars
Preparation Time: 15 minutes

These high-calorie bars are meant to replace the costly high-carbohydrate, high-protein energy bars used by athletes.

- ½ cup honey
- ½ cup cooked brown rice
- ½ cup peanut butter (chunky or smooth)
- ½ cup sesame seeds
- ½ cup dried fruit
- 1½ cups oats
- 1 cup powdered milk
- ¼ cup sweetened shredded coconut

In a blender or food processor, blend the honey and brown rice until few lumps of rice are left. Pour into a mixing bowl and mix in the peanut butter and sesame seeds with a mixer. Put the dried fruit into the blender, and blend until the fruit is in small pieces. Add the fruit into the mix. Add the oats, powdered milk, and coconut, and work into the dough. If necessary, mix the stiff dough by hand.

Press the dough evenly into a greased 8x12 pan. Cut into 8 squares. Wrap each square in plastic wrap. Store in the refrigerator if you are not planning to eat this within a week. They will last 1 to 2 months if covered airtight in the refrigerator.

Option: Replace the fruit with chocolate chips or chopped nuts.

Cost per serving (1 bar): 44¢

NUTRITIONAL ANALYSIS PER SERVING

Calories: 468

Fat: 21 grams

Cholesterol: 16 mg

Carbohydrates: 59 grams

Fiber: 2 grams

Protein: 16 grams

Sodium: 150 mg

Kitchen Tip

To MEASURE HONEY, molasses, or corn syrup without leaving a good deal of it on the measuring spoon or cup, spray the measuring tool with cooking oil spray or rub a little oil on it first. The honey will come right off and you will get a more accurate amount into your recipe. If honey is in a recipe where oil is also called for, measure the oil first and then the honey.

Fruit Crisp

Serves 4
Preparation Time: 15 minutes
Cooking Time: 20 minutes

- 3 cups diced fresh or canned fruit (apples, peaches, cherries, berries)
- ½ cup flour
- ½ cup rolled oats
- ¼ cup brown sugar
- 2 T. sugar
- ½ tsp. cinnamon
- ¼ tsp. nutmeg
- ¼ tsp. salt
- 4 T. cold butter

NUTRITIONAL ANALYSIS PER SERVING
Calories: 300
Fat: 12 grams
Cholesterol: 31 mg
Carbohydrates: 46 grams
Fiber: 3 grams
Protein: 4 grams
Sodium: 254 mg

Spread the fruit in a bread loaf pan or an 8x8 pan, distributing evenly.

In a separate mixing bowl, combine the rest of the ingredients with a pastry blender until the butter is evenly mixed in. Crumble the topping over the fruit.

Bake at 350° for 20 minutes or until the topping is golden brown.

Variation: Add chopped nuts to the topping for added flavor and texture.

Cost per serving (1 cup): 13¢

 *Kitchen Tip*

A PASTRY BLENDER is a small, hand-held, inexpensive wire gadget for cutting butter and shortening into dry ingredients. You can get similar results by using two knives or a fork. It works best if the butter is hard.

Graham Cracker Toffee

Serves 24
Preparation Time: 15 minutes
Cooking Time: 8 minutes

- 12 honey graham cracker sheets (1 inner package)
- ½ cup butter
- ½ cup vegetable oil
- ½ cup brown sugar
- 1 cup chopped nuts (any type)

Line a cookie sheet with foil. Break up each sheet of crackers into the 4 individual crackers. Place the graham crackers on the foil-lined pan in a single layer.

In a 2-qt. saucepan bring the butter, oil, and brown sugar to a boil over very low heat, stirring constantly. Once the sugar is dissolved, remove from heat and add the nuts. Mix well, then pour over the crackers, spreading it evenly.

Bake at 400° for 7 to 8 minutes, or until the topping is bubbling. Check on these every few minutes, as they can burn easily.

Variation: Use chocolate graham crackers instead of plain.

Cost per serving (2 crackers): 14¢

NUTRITIONAL ANALYSIS PER SERVING	
Calories: 154	
Fat: 12 grams	
Cholesterol: 10 mg	
Carbohydrates: 10 grams	
Fiber: 1 gram	
Protein: 1 gram	
Sodium: 86 mg	

 *Kitchen Tip*

Sylvester Graham, a Presbyterian minister and physiologist, invented GRAHAM CRACKERS in 1830 as a snack. Graham flour is whole wheat flour that is more coarsely ground than flour used in baking bread.

Chocolate Meringue Drops

Makes 28 cookies
Preparation Time: 10 minutes
Cooking Time: 10 minutes

- 2 egg whites
- 1¼ cups powdered sugar
- 3 T. unsweetened cocoa powder
- 1 T. flour
- ½ T. water

Beat the egg whites with a mixer until frothy but not stiff. Turn the mixer to low and add the powdered sugar, cocoa powder, flour, and water. Once blended, turn the speed to high and beat until the mixture is thick.

Drop the mixture by heaping teaspoons onto baking sheets. Bake at 350° for 10 minutes or until the top of each cookie cracks slightly. Let the cookies cool completely (about 10 minutes) without disturbing them.

These cookies should be eaten the same day they are baked. They do not store well—they become chewy instead of crisp.

Option: For white meringue cookies, omit the chocolate. You can also add ½ cup finely chopped nuts to either recipe.

Cost per serving (1 cookie): 3¢

NUTRITIONAL ANALYSIS PER SERVING
Calories: 24
Fat: 0 grams
Cholesterol: 0 mg
Carbohydrates: 6 grams
Fiber: 0 grams
Protein: 0 grams
Sodium: 4 mg

Kitchen Tip

MERINGUE is a mixture of stiffly beaten egg whites and sugar. Meringues can be soft or hard depending on how soft or hard the egg white peaks are. Meringue is used for cookies (as above) or as a coating for desserts (e.g. baked Alaska). Meringue powder is used to create a meringue texture in icing without having to beat the egg whites.

Berry Cobbler

Serves 6
Preparation Time: 15 minutes
Cooking Time: 30 minutes

Filling:

- 4 cups fresh or frozen berries (blueberries, raspberries, blackberries, or boysenberries)*
- ½ cup brown sugar
- 2 T. whole wheat flour
- ½ tsp. lemon juice
- 1 T. water

*My favorite combination of berries is 2 cups blueberries with 2 cups blackberries.

Crust:

- 3 T. cold butter
- 1 cup whole wheat flour
- ¼ cup brown sugar
- 1½ tsp. baking powder
- ½ tsp. salt
- ⅔ cup low-fat milk

In a small saucepan, combine the berries, brown sugar, flour, lemon juice, and water. Heat over medium heat, stirring constantly. Once a thick sauce forms, remove from heat, and pour into a greased 2-qt. baking dish or bread pan.

In a large mixing bowl, make the crust by cutting the butter into the flour with a pastry blender until the mixture is fine and crumbly. Add the brown sugar, baking powder, and salt, and mix. Stir in the milk to form a sticky dough. Drop dough by spoonfuls onto the berry mixture, covering all the berries. If desired, sprinkle the crust with 2 teaspoons granulated sugar. Bake at 400° for 25 to 30 minutes or until the crust is golden brown. If desired, serve warm with vanilla ice cream.

Cost per serving (1¼ cup): 51¢

NUTRITIONAL ANALYSIS PER SERVING
Calories: 189
Fat: 7 grams
Cholesterol: 16 mg
Carbohydrates: 31 grams
Fiber: 5 grams
Protein: 4 grams
Sodium: 342 mg

 Kitchen Tip

To keep ICE CRYSTALS from forming in your ice cream, don't store the ice cream in the door of the freezer—the temperature fluctuates too much in that area. When ice cream melts and refreezes, ice crystals form.

Christmas Toffee

Serves 8
Preparation Time: 1 hour, 15 minutes

- ½ cup butter
- 1½ cups brown sugar
- 4 oz. (¼ cup) slivered almonds
- ¼ tsp. salt
- 1 cup chocolate chips, divided
- ¼ cup finely chopped walnuts, divided

Melt the butter over medium heat in a 2-qt. saucepan. Add the brown sugar, stir, and bring to a gentle boil. Heat until the temperature reaches 310° on a candy thermometer to form a hard ball.

Immediately remove from heat and stir in the almonds. Pour the almond mix onto a baking sheet lined with waxed paper, and spread the mixture evenly. While the candy is still hot, sprinkle ½ cup of the chocolate chips over the candy. The heat from the candy will melt them and make it easy to spread them evenly over the candy with a knife. Sprinkle 2 tablespoons of the walnuts evenly over the melted chocolate. Let the candy cool for 20 minutes in the refrigerator or 1 hour at room temperature.

Once cooled, turn the candy over so the chocolate side is on the bottom. Peel off the paper. Place the other ½ cup chocolate chips in a small bowl, and melt in the microwave. Drizzle the chocolate over the candy, and then sprinkle with the other 2 tablespoons walnuts. Once the chocolate is hardened, break up the candy (I use a wooden kitchen mallet).

Cost per serving (⅓ cup): 39¢

NUTRITIONAL ANALYSIS PER SERVING	
Calories: 335	
Fat: 20 grams	
Cholesterol: 31 mg	
Carbohydrates: 41 grams	
Fiber: 2 grams	
Protein: 2 grams	
Sodium: 196 mg	

Kitchen Tip

To easily CRUSH NUTS, place them in a sealed plastic bag, and roll with a rolling pin until the nuts are the desired size.

Cinnamon Crispies

Serves 8
Preparation Time: 5 minutes
Cooking Time: 10 minutes

- 2 T. cinnamon
- ½ cup sugar
- 6 fat-free flour tortillas, taco size
- cooking oil spray

In a small bowl, mix the cinnamon and sugar, and set aside.

Cut each tortilla into 6 wedges, like you would cut a pizza. Lay them on a baking sheet. Spray lightly with cooking oil spray. Bake at 350° for 3 minutes, watching carefully so they don't burn.

Flip them over, spray and cook the other side in the same manner. Take them out of the oven and immediately sprinkle the tortillas with the sugar mixture. Serve while warm.

Cost per serving (4 to 5 wedges): 13¢

NUTRITIONAL ANALYSIS PER SERVING
Calories: 150
Fat: 2 grams
Cholesterol: 0 mg
Carbohydrates: 30 grams
Fiber: 2 grams
Protein: 3 grams
Sodium: 271 mg

Kitchen Tip

To make a grander dessert, SAUTÉ SLICED APPLES or peaches in butter and cinnamon sugar. Serve with the cinnamon crispies.

Gummie Squares

Makes 80 candies
Preparation Time: 5 minutes
Chilling Time: 4 hours

- 3 envelopes unflavored gelatin
- 1 cup boiling water
- 2 cups sugar
- ¼ cup orange or cranberry juice
- 6 drops any color food coloring

Dissolve the gelatin in the boiling water. Stir in the sugar until the sugar is dissolved. Once dissolved, add the fruit juice and food coloring.

Pour into plastic candy molds or into an 8x12 pan. Place in the refrigerator for 3 to 4 hours or until set.

Turn the candies out of the molds (if needed, gently use the pointed end of a sharp knife to aid them, or run warm water over the back of the mold for 15 seconds to loosen). To release from the pan, loosen the sides of the gelatin with a spatula and turn out onto a greased cooking sheet. Cut into 1-inch cubes with a sharp knife. If the knife begins to stick to the candy, run the knife under hot water (dry it off before cutting). If desired, roll in sugar.

Option: For sour candy, roll them in ascorbic acid instead of sugar. Ascorbic acid is sold in health food stores as powdered vitamin C.

Cost per serving (4 candies): 22¢

NUTRITIONAL ANALYSIS PER SERVING	
Calories: 83	
Fat: 0 grams	
Cholesterol: 0 mg	
Carbohydrates: 20 grams	
Fiber: 0 grams	
Protein: 2 grams	
Sodium: 1 mg	

Kitchen Tip

In 1890, Charles Knox developed the world's first granulated GELATIN. Prior to developing his formula, the only way to make gelatin was a long and difficult process. As his granulated gelatin gained recognition with cooks, gelatin-based dishes began to gain popularity.

Cosmic Caramel Corn

Serves 12
Preparation Time: 10 minutes
Cooking Time: 5 minutes

- 1½ cups popcorn kernels (about 15 to 20 cups popped popcorn)
- ½ cup butter
- 1 cup sugar
- 1 cup brown sugar
- 1 can sweetened condensed milk

Pop the popcorn and pour it into a very large mixing bowl.

Melt the butter over medium heat in a 1-quart saucepan. Add the sugars and milk. Mix well and bring to a boil. Stir constantly while it boils for 2 to 3 minutes. Remove from heat. Pour ⅓ of the sauce over the popcorn, and mix in. Pour another ⅓ in, and mix. Then pour the rest, and mix.

For a delicate crispy coating, let the caramel corn dry, uncovered, for 4 to 6 hours (or even overnight). Then store in an airtight container in a dry place (not the refrigerator).

Cost per serving (1½ cups): 36¢

NUTRITIONAL ANALYSIS PER SERVING	
Calories: 345	
Fat: 12 grams	
Cholesterol: 35 mg	
Carbohydrates: 60 grams	
Fiber: 1 gram	
Protein: 3 grams	
Sodium: 153 mg	

 *Kitchen Tip*

POPCORN KERNELS vary in size once popped. One cup of kernels can make anywhere from 8 cups to 20 cups of popcorn, depending on the kernel quality.

Cracker Faddle

Serves 8
Preparation Time: 10 minutes
Cooking Time: 20 minutes

- ¾ cup sugar
- ½ cup brown sugar
- ½ cup water
- ½ cup butter
- ½ cup light corn syrup
- ½ tsp. salt
- ½ tsp. vanilla
- 6 cups popped popcorn (unbuttered)
- ½ cup nuts (almonds or peanuts are best)

In a large saucepan, combine the sugars, water, butter, corn syrup, and salt. Heat to boiling while covered; continue boiling (watch that it doesn't bubble over) for 5 to 10 minutes or until the syrup reaches 275° on a candy thermometer, or the soft-ball stage. (See "The Miserly Kitchen" chapter.) Remove from heat and add the vanilla.

Distribute the popcorn over a large nonstick cookie sheet. Drizzle the syrup over the popcorn as evenly as possible. Stir to mix it. Bake at 350° for 5 minutes or until the syrup is bubbling. Remove from oven, sprinkle the nuts over the popcorn, and stir again. Let candy cool and harden. Break into pieces, and store in an airtight container.

Cost per serving (1 cup): 29¢

NUTRITIONAL ANALYSIS PER SERVING
Calories: 270
Fat: 17 grams
Cholesterol: 31 mg
Carbohydrates: 31 grams
Fiber: 2 grams
Protein: 2 grams
Sodium: 279 mg

 *Kitchen Tip*

CORN SYRUP is a thick sweetener that is made by processing cornstarch with acids. It is preferred for making candies because it does not crystallize over time like sugar-based syrups. It comes in light and dark forms: light has been filtered to remove impurities; dark has caramel coloring and flavoring added.

No-Bake Cookies

Makes 18 cookies
Preparation Time: 15 minutes

- 2 cups sugar
- ½ cup cocoa powder, unsweetened
- ½ cup butter
- ½ cup low-fat milk
- 3 cups oats
- ½ tsp. salt
- 1 tsp. vanilla

NUTRITIONAL ANALYSIS PER SERVING
Calories: 240
Fat: 7 grams
Cholesterol: 14 mg
Carbohydrates: 41 grams
Fiber: 1 gram
Protein: 5 grams
Sodium: 115 mg

Place the sugar, cocoa, butter, and milk in a medium saucepan and mix. Cook over medium heat, bringing it to a boil while stirring constantly. Let boil for 5 minutes while stirring.

Remove from heat. Add the oats, salt, and vanilla to the sauce, and stir to mix. Scoop by heaping tablespoons onto waxed paper or parchment. Let cool. Store in an airtight container.

Cost per serving (1 cookie): 12¢

 *Kitchen Tip*

OATS are one of the most nutritious of all cereal grains. The grain comes in many forms: groats, Scotch, steel-cut, Irish, rolled, instant, and quick. Groats have the hull removed and the kernel toasted. They have the appearance of rice kernels and can be cooked and served as rice is. Scotch, Irish, and steel-cut oats are groats that have been chopped into small pieces. Rolled oats are steamed groats that are pressed with giant rollers, so they cook quicker. Rolled oats are also called old-fashioned oats. Instant oats are very thin precooked oats. They should never be used where rolled or old-fashioned oats are called for. Quick rolled oats are not the same as instant oats, but are groats that have been cut up into small pieces before being rolled.

Quick Peanut Butter Cookies

Makes 6 cookies
Preparation Time: 5 minutes
Cooking Time: 10 minutes

- 1 cup peanut butter (creamy works best)
- 1 cup sugar
- 1 egg

Place peanut butter in a large microwave-safe bowl. Warm the peanut butter on low heat in the microwave until it is very soft (1 to 2 minutes). Add the sugar, and mix well, then add the egg. Mix until smooth. Roll into balls 1 inch in diameter, and place on an ungreased cooking sheet. Bake at 350° for 8 to 10 minutes or until golden.

These are best served warm!

Cost per serving (1 cookie): 15¢

NUTRITIONAL ANALYSIS PER SERVING
Calories: 196
Fat: 11 grams
Cholesterol: 15 mg
Carbohydrates: 21 grams
Fiber: 1 gram
Protein: 6 grams
Sodium: 106 mg

Kitchen Tip

PEANUT BUTTER was invented in 1890 by blending ground peanuts with oil and salt. Some manufacturers also add sugar and additives to keep the peanut butter from separating from the oil. Creamy peanut butter has been ground very fine and is only available with added ingredients. Chunky peanut butter is creamy peanut butter with chopped nuts added back in. "Natural" peanut butter is made from only ground peanuts. It is stiffer, and its natural oil separates, so it needs to be mixed into the peanuts before each use.

Hi-Fiber Cookies

Makes 18 cookies
Preparation Time: 15 minutes
Cooking Time: 10 minutes

- ½ cup whole wheat flour
- ¼ cup white flour
- ¾ cup oats
- ¾ cup oat bran
- ½ cup wheat germ
- ½ tsp. baking soda
- ¼ tsp. salt
- ¼ tsp. cinnamon
- ¼ tsp. nutmeg
- ½ cup brown sugar
- 1 egg, beaten
- 3 T. oil
- ½ cup low-fat milk

NUTRITIONAL ANALYSIS PER SERVING
Calories: 105
Fat: 4 grams
Cholesterol: 10 mg
Carbohydrates: 17 grams
Fiber: 2 grams
Protein: 4 grams
Sodium: 73 mg

Place all of the ingredients in a mixing bowl, and mix until well blended. Drop by heaping table-spoons onto a greased baking sheet. Flatten each cookie by pressing with the back of a fork. Bake at 350° for 10 minutes.

Store in an airtight container.

Option: Add ½ cup raisins, dried cranberries, chopped nuts, chopped dates, or sunflower seeds with the other ingredients.

Cost per serving (1 cookie): 6¢

Kitchen Tip

WHEAT GERM is the heart of the wheat kernel. It is where the most vitamins are stored, including a high content of vitamin E. Wheat germ oil is extracted from this portion. Wheat germ should be stored in the refrigerator to keep the oils in the wheat germ from becoming rancid.

Slim Mint Chocolate Cookies

Makes 80 cookies
Preparation Time: 15 minutes
Chilling Time: 2 hours
Cooking Time: 10 minutes

Dough:

- 18 oz. devil's food or chocolate fudge cake mix
- 3 T. butter, melted
- ½ cup flour
- 1 egg
- ¼ cup water
- ¼ tsp. peppermint extract

Coating:

- ¼ tsp. peppermint extract
- 6 T. butter
- 4 cups semi-sweet chocolate chips

In a large mixing bowl, combine the dough ingredients. Mix by hand until a crumbly dough forms. Roll the dough into 4 logs about 1½ inches in diameter. Wrap in plastic wrap and refrigerate for 2 hours.

Remove wrapping, and slice logs into ¼-inch cookie rounds. Bake on a greased nonstick baking sheet at 350° for 10 minutes. Remove the cookies from the baking sheet immediately after removing from the oven, and cool on a cooling rack.

Place the coating ingredients in a double boiler (see Kitchen Tip) over medium heat, and melt, stirring frequently. Add a bit of water (1 tablespoon at a time) if it thickens too much. Once melted, remove chocolate from the heat and dip cookies one at a time into the chocolate, then place on a cooling rack to dry. Placing the rack in the refrigerator will speed up cooling time. Once dry, store in an airtight container.

Cost per serving (2 cookies): 17¢

NUTRITIONAL ANALYSIS PER SERVING	
Calories: 161	
Fat: 9 grams	
Cholesterol: 11 mg	
Carbohydrates: 21 grams	
Fiber: 1 gram	
Protein: 2 grams	
Sodium: 111 mg	

Kitchen Tip

COOKIES were invented centuries ago when refined sugar became available. The word *cookie* comes from a Dutch word that means "little cake." Most cookies contain flour, shortening, and sugar, although some exceptions to that recipe exist, like the one above.

Watermelon Sorbet

Serves 4
Preparation Time: 5 minutes
Freezing Time: 1 to 2 hours

- 2 cups cubed, seedless watermelon
- ½ tsp. lemon juice
- 2 T. honey

Place all of the ingredients in a blender. Blend until smooth. Pour into an 8x8 baking dish. Freeze uncovered for 1 to 2 hours or until firm but pliable. If freezing overnight, let soften at room temperature before serving.

To serve, scoop into bowls.

Cost per serving (½ cup): 30¢

NUTRITIONAL ANALYSIS PER SERVING
Calories: 46
Fat: 0 grams
Cholesterol: 0 mg
Carbohydrates: 12 grams
Fiber: 0 grams
Protein: 0 grams
Sodium: 1 mg

Kitchen Tip

LEFTOVER WATERMELON that is overripe can be used in recipes like the one above or blended with sugar and frozen in Popsicle molds. Other fruit can be used in place of watermelon, but watermelon has the best texture for these types of recipes.

Hot Fudge Sauce

Makes 1½ cups
Preparation Time: 5 minutes
Cooking Time: 10 minutes

- ½ cup cocoa powder, unsweetened
- 1¼ cups sugar
- ¼ tsp. salt
- ½ cup milk
- ¼ cup butter
- 1 tsp. vanilla

In a 1-qt. saucepan, combine the cocoa, sugar, and salt. Mix together until no cocoa lumps remain. Add the milk and butter, and stir. Place over medium heat, and stir occasionally until the butter is melted. Once the butter melts, stir constantly until the sugar is dissolved (but do not boil), then remove from heat. Stir in the vanilla once syrup is cool.

Store in a covered jar in the refrigerator for 2 to 3 months. It will become very thick when it is cold, but thins out when reheated (use low heat and stir constantly).

Use as an ice cream topping, as a dip for sliced fruit, or as a topping for brownies.

Variation: For a mint fudge sauce, add ½ teaspoon peppermint extract with the vanilla.

Cost per serving (¼ cup): 12¢

NUTRITIONAL ANALYSIS PER SERVING
Calories: 258
Fat: 9 grams
Cholesterol: 23 mg
Carbohydrates: 47 grams
Fiber: 2 grams
Protein: 2 grams
Sodium: 134 mg

 Kitchen Tip

VANILLA is made from the fruit of a rare variety of orchid. The thin pod, which resembles a bean, is dried for six months. To make vanilla extract, the beans are chopped and soaked in an alcohol solution for several months. To make vanilla flavored sugar, place a vanilla bean in a container of sugar for a few days. The sugar absorbs the vanilla flavor. Discard the bean, and use the sugar as an elegant addition to coffee or tea.

Chocolate Syrup

(like Hershey's Syrup)

Makes 3 cups
Preparation Time: 5 minutes
Cooking Time: 10 minutes

- 1 cup cocoa powder, unsweetened
- 2 cups sugar
- ¼ tsp. salt
- 1¼ cups water
- 1 T. vanilla

NUTRITIONAL ANALYSIS PER SERVING	
Calories: 147	
Fat: 1 gram	
Cholesterol: 0 mg	
Carbohydrates: 37 grams	
Fiber: 2 grams	
Protein: 1 gram	
Sodium: 47 mg	

In a 1-qt. saucepan, combine the cocoa, sugar, and salt. Mix together until no cocoa lumps remain. Add the water, and stir. Place over medium heat, and stir occasionally until the sugar is dissolved (but do not boil), then remove from heat. Stir in the vanilla once syrup is cool.

Store in a covered jar in the refrigerator for 2 to 3 months. It will become very thick when it is cold, but thins when reheated (use low heat and stir constantly). This can be stored at room temperature for one month.

Use as ice cream topping, in milk to make chocolate milk, or in coffee to make coffee mocha.

Cost per serving (¼ cup): 11¢

Kitchen Tip

Cooks use several TYPES OF CHOCOLATE: BAKING CHOCOLATE (also known as bitter or unsweetened) has no sugar added to the roasted ground cocoa bean; UNSWEETENED COCOA POWDER is a residue after squeezing most of the fat out of the ground cocoa bean; BITTERSWEET (also know as semi-sweet) is the ground cocoa bean with added sugar; MILK CHOCOLATE is ground cocoa bean plus sugar and milk; WHITE CHOCOLATE is not a chocolate product, but is a combination of sugar, shortening, milk, and vanilla.

Flavored Cream Cheese

Serves 6
Preparation Time: 5 minutes

- 3 oz. low-fat cream cheese, softened at room temperature
- 2 tsp. jam, any flavor

Place the cream cheese and jam in a mixing bowl. Blend with a mixer on low speed until it is smooth and well blended. Spread on a bagel or toast.

Store in an airtight container in the refrigerator for 7 to 10 days.

Variations: Substitute the same amount of one of these ingredients for the jam: diced smoked salmon, herbs, chives, crushed pineapple, etc.

Cost per serving (1 T.): 11¢

NUTRITIONAL ANALYSIS PER SERVING	
Calories: 38	
Fat: 3 grams	
Cholesterol: 8 mg	
Carbohydrates: 2 grams	
Fiber: 0 grams	
Protein: 2 grams	
Sodium: 43 mg	

 Kitchen Tip

CREAM CHEESE is a soft cheese made from milk, cream, and starter bacteria. It is very high in fat (usually 33%) but does come in a low-fat version, usually thickened with guar gum or gelatin to achieve the texture of a higher fat cheese. It can be stored in an airtight container in the refrigerator for one week after opening.

Rice Pudding

Serves 4
Preparation Time: 5 minutes
Cooking Time: 30 minutes

- 1 cup cooked rice (this is a great use for left-over rice)
- 1 tsp. vanilla extract
- ¼ tsp. cinnamon
- 2 eggs
- ¼ cup sugar
- ¼ cup milk

Combine all of the ingredients in a mixing bowl and mix well. Pour into a greased loaf pan. Bake at 325° for 20–30 minutes or until the center is firm.

Serve warm. Drizzle honey over the top for added flavor.

Option: Add ½ cup raisins to the batter before mixing, and drizzle butterscotch sauce (see next page) instead of honey.

Cost per serving (¾ cup): 5¢

NUTRITIONAL ANALYSIS PER SERVING	
Calories: 154	
Fat: 2 grams	
Cholesterol: 91 mg	
Carbohydrates: 28 grams	
Fiber: 0 grams	
Protein: 5 grams	
Sodium: 36 mg	

Kitchen Tip

EGGS must always be stored in the refrigerator. They are best when used within a week of purchase but can be stored for up to a month (check expiration date). When stored at room temperature, they lose flavor and texture seven times faster than if stored in the refrigerator. They should be stored large end up, and never put near something with a strong odor (eggs are very absorbent).

Butterscotch Sauce

Makes 2¾ cups
Preparation Time: 3 minutes
Cooking Time: 5 minutes

- 1½ cups light brown sugar
- ½ cup corn syrup
- ⅔ cup half-and-half

In a 1-qt. saucepan, combine the brown sugar and corn syrup. Stir to mix well. Place over medium heat, and stir occasionally until the sugar is dissolved, then remove from heat. Stir in the half-and-half.

Store in a covered jar in the refrigerator for 1 to 2 months. It will become very thick when it is cold, but thins out when reheated (use low heat and stir constantly).

Use as an ice cream topping, as a dip for sliced fruit, or as a topping for brownies.

Note: For an even richer sauce, replace the half-and-half with heavy whipping cream. For a sauce that is less rich, use evaporated milk instead.

Cost per serving (¼ cup): 17¢

NUTRITIONAL ANALYSIS PER SERVING	
Calories: 180	
Fat: 5 grams	
Cholesterol: 20 mg	
Carbohydrates: 35 grams	
Fiber: 0 grams	
Protein: 0 grams	
Sodium: 37 mg	

Kitchen Tip

HEAVY WHIPPING CREAM is the same thing as HEAVY CREAM. It has the highest fat content of all the creams (36% or more). It is not to be used interchangeably in recipes with WHIPPING CREAM (30 to 36% fat), TABLE CREAM (18 to 30% fat), or HALF-AND-HALF. Half-and-half is half cream and half milk. Its fat content (10 to 18%) is the lowest of all of the creams and prevents it from whipping into whipped cream. Use heavy whipping cream, heavy cream, or whipping cream to make whipped cream.

CHAPTER 14

FOOD STORAGE CHART

Proper freezer storage requires proper wrapping. When wrapping food for freezing, burp the air out of the wrapping, and seal well. Air causes freezer burn and increases the spoilage rate. It's a good idea to double-wrap most foods to assure air does not get to it.

The following chart indicates the maximum suggested storage time for a variety of foods. If a column is blank, freezing or refrigeration is not a recommended storage method.

Food	Pantry	Refrigerator	Freezer
MILK			
Condensed, unopened	12 months		
Condensed, opened		1 week	
Powdered, unopened	6 months		
Powdered, opened	3 months		
Opened homogenized		1 week	
Unopened homogenized		1 to 2 weeks	1 month
Sour cream		2 weeks	2 months
Butter		1 to 2 weeks	6–9 months
Margarine		4–6 months	12 months
CHEESE			
Cheddar, Swiss, etc., unopened		3–6 months	6 to 8 months

Food	Pantry	Refrigerator	Freezer
Cottage		1 week	3 months
Cream cheese		2 weeks	3 months
Grated Parmesan		2 months	6 to 8 months
EGGS			
In shell		2 to 3 weeks	
Out of shell		3 days	12 months
Hard-boiled		1 week	
PRODUCE			
Fruit, fresh, uncut		1 to 3 weeks	
Fruit, fresh, cut up		1 week	12 months
Vegetables, fresh, uncut		3 to 5 days	
Vegetables, fresh, cut up		1 to 3 days	8 months
Canned vegetables, opened		2 to 3 days	
Canned fruit, opened		1 week	
BREADS			
Dough		1 to 3 days	10 months
Loaf, baked	3 to 5 days	1 to 2 weeks	2 to 4 months
Bread crumbs, fresh		1 to 2 weeks	6 months
Bread crumbs, dried	6 months	8 months	12 months
CONDIMENTS			
Mayonnaise, opened		2 months	
Mayonnaise, unopened	2 to 3 months		
Honey	12 months		12 months
Jam, jelly, unopened	12 months		
Jam, jelly, opened		10 months	
Herbs, dried	12 months		

Food	Pantry	Refrigerator	Freezer
Salad dressing, bottled, unopened	12 months		
Salad dressing, bottled, opened		3 months	
Salad dressing, made from mix, opened		2 weeks	
Ketchup, unopened	12 months		
Ketchup, opened	1 month	6 months	
MEAT			
Fish			3–6 months
Shrimp, uncooked			12 months
Lunch meat, opened		3 to 5 days	
Lunch meat, unopened		2 weeks	1 to 2 months
Meat and chicken, fresh		3 to 5 days	6–12 months
Meat leftovers, cooked		3 to 4 days	2 to 3 months
Gravy/broth		1 to 2 days	2 to 3 months
Soup or stew		3 to 4 days	2 to 3 months
BAKING			
Flour, white	15 months		
Flour, whole wheat	5 months		
Baking powder	12 months		
Bouillon cube/powder	12 months		
Chocolate	12 months		
Cooking oils	12 months		
Peanut butter	6 months		
Sugar	2 years		
Brown sugar	4 months		
Dry mixes	8 to 10 months		
Vanilla extract	12 months		

MEASURING ABBREVIATIONS

lb.	=	pound
mg	=	milligram
oz.	=	ounce
qt.	=	quart
T.	=	tablespoon
tsp.	=	teaspoon

FOOD EQUIVALENCY CHART

Cooking Conversions

Food	Dry Amount	After Cooking
Dried beans	1¼ cups	3 cups
Macaroni	1 cup	2¼ cups
Macaroni	1 pound	9 cups
Noodles, egg	3 cups	4 cups
Noodles, egg	1 pound	8 cups
Rice, regular	1 cup	3½ cups
Rice, instant	1 cup	2 cups
Spaghetti	1 pound	9 cups
Spaghetti	7 oz.	4 cups

EMERGENCY SUBSTITUTIONS

Food Needed	What to Do
Baking powder, 1 tsp.	¼ tsp. baking soda + ½ tsp. cream of tartar
Buttermilk, 1 cup	1 cup milk + 1 T. vinegar
Cornstarch, 1 T.	2 T. flour
Garlic, 1 clove	⅛ tsp. powdered garlic
Half-and-half, 1 cup	⅞ cup milk + 3 T. melted butter
Heavy cream, 1 cup	¾ cup milk + ⅓ cup melted butter
Herb, fresh, 1 T.	1 tsp. dried
Honey, 1 cup	1 cup sugar + ¼ cup water
Milk, whole, 1 cup	1 cup skim milk + 2 tsp. melted butter
Onion, ¼ cup	1 tsp. powdered onion or 1 T. dried minced onion

Unsweetened baking chocolate, 1 oz.	3 T. cocoa powder + 1 T. butter or ¼ cup semi-sweet chocolate chips and remove 2 tsp. sugar from recipe
Semi-sweet chocolate, 1 oz.	1 T. unsweetened chocolate square + 1 T. sugar
Yeast, cake	1 pkg. or 2 tsp. dry yeast

MEASURING CONVERSIONS

(Quantities are approximate)

Food	Weight	Amount
Banana	3 whole	1 cup mashed
Butter	1 pound	2 cups
Carrots, raw	1 pound	4 cups sliced
Celery	1 rib	¾ cup sliced
Cheese, grated	4 oz.	1 cup
Cheese, grated Parmesan	3 oz.	1 cup
Chicken, cooked	1½ pounds	2 cups cubed
Chocolate chips	6 oz.	1 cup
Cocoa powder	4 oz.	1 cup
Coffee	1 pound	88 T.
Cornmeal	1 pound	2⅔ cups
Flour, white	1 pound	4 cups
Flour, whole wheat	1 pound	3½ cups
Honey	1 pound	1⅓ cups
Lemon juice	1 lemon	3 to 4 T.
Nuts	2 oz.	½ cup
Oats, uncooked	1 pound	5⅓ cups
Onions, green	1 whole	2 T. chopped
Onions, yellow	1 whole	1 cup chopped
Parsley	1 bunch	1½ cups chopped
Popcorn kernels	1 cup	8–20 cups popped
Potatoes, mashed	1 whole	½ cup mashed

Potatoes, raw	1 pound	1½ cups diced
Powdered milk	⅜ cup	2 cups prepared
Spinach, fresh	1 pound	1½ cups cooked
Strawberries	1 pound	1¾ cups sliced
Sugar, brown	1 pound	2¼ cups
Sugar, granulated	1 pound	2 cups
Sugar, powdered	1 pound	4½ cups
Zucchini, medium	1 whole	1 cup grated

WEIGHTS AND MEASURES

This may come in handy if you want to make more or less of a recipe or mix.

1 gallon	=	4 quarts						
1 quart	=	2 pints						
1 pint	=	2 cups						
1 cup	=	8 oz.	=	16 T.	=	48 tsp.	=	237 ml.
¾ cup	=	6 oz.	=	12 T.	=	36 tsp.	=	177 ml.
⅔ cup	=	5 oz.	=	11 T.	=	32 tsp.	=	158 ml.
½ cup	=	4 oz.	=	8 T.	=	24 tsp.	=	118 ml.
⅓ cup	=	3 oz.	=	5 T.	=	16 tsp.	=	79 ml.
¼ cup	=	2 oz.	=	4 T.	=	12 tsp.	=	59 ml.
⅛ cup	=	1 oz.	=	2 T.	=	6 tsp.	=	30 ml.
1⁄16 cup	=	.5 oz.	=	1 T.	=	3 tsp.	=	15 ml.

METRIC CONVERSION CHART

Volume		U.S. Units		Metric Units
1 teaspoon	=	1/6 ounce	=	5 milliliters
1 tablespoon	=	0.5 ounce	=	15 milliliters
1 fluid ounce	=	1 ounce	=	30 milliliters
1 cup	=	8 ounces	=	237 milliliters

General Index

Recipe Index

Kitchen Tips Index

Save More With Jonni McCoy!

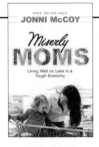

Full of tips, tactics, and recipes, *Miserly Moms* introduces the tried-and-true Eleven Miserly Guidelines that can save you thousands of dollars a year! Completely practical and easy to do, they reveal how to

- save money on groceries,
- see through warehouse clubs' "deals,"
- celebrate holidays without breaking your budget, and
- spot sneaky marketing tricks.

In simple, everyday ways, you and your family can save money and still live well in a tough economy.

Miserly Moms by Jonni McCoy